CENTRE COURT

THE JEWEL IN WIMBLEDON'S CROWN

CENTRE COURT

THE JEWEL IN WIMBLEDON'S CROWN

 The All England Lawn Tennis & Croquet Club

Edited by John Barrett and Ian Hewitt

ACKNOWLEDGEMENTS

This book is the product of many contributors.

We have, thankfully, called heavily upon the knowledge and research of Alan Little (our Honorary Librarian) whose *Wimbledon Compendium* remains a definitive source of information along with his delightful books *Wimbledon 1922: The New Ground and The Centre Court* and *Wimbledon: The Changing Face of Church Road* both published by Wimbledon Lawn Tennis Museum. Similarly, we are very grateful to Honor Godfrey (Museum Curator) and her team for their assistance. The Museum and its treasures have provided much fascinating source material. We also thank Chris Gorringe (the Club's former Chief Executive) for his guidance during the early stages of the project.

The various pieces on the Great Champions are derived from two books written by John Barrett and Alan Little (with earlier contributions from Lance Tingay). Published by Wimbledon Lawn Tennis Museum, they are *Wimbledon Ladies' Singles Champions 1884-2004* and *Wimbledon Gentlemen's Singles Champions 1877-2005* respectively.

Edited reports on the Memorable Matches have been extracted from articles published at the time and we thank the various newspapers for permission to use them.

Photographs have been vital to reflect the life and drama of the Centre Court. Most have come from the Club's own archive (where the research of Rosabel Richards has been invaluable) and many are previously unpublished. Photographs from the family collection of Michael Cole have added significantly to the book. We thank Bob Martin, our photographic editor, and his team – Tom Lovelock, Neil Tingle and Tommy Hindley/Professional Sport – for their stunning contributions, and we congratulate the publishers, Vision Sports Publishing, on bringing our ideas so creatively to fruition.

John Barrett and Ian Hewitt, May 2010

CONTENTS

THE ROYAL BOX	187		
GREAT DOUBLES PAIRS	199		
PLAY IS SUSPENDED	211		
PLAY RESUMES	223		
QUIET PLEASE!	241		

MEMORABLE MATCHES

Running chronologically through the pages of this book, between each chapter, are edited reports of the following 39 memorable Centre Court matches, described by leading tennis writers of the day. We are especially grateful to the newspapers concerned for allowing us to reproduce their material.

FOREWORD BY
ROGER FEDERER

I AM DELIGHTED to support this splendid book by the All England Club celebrating the history of Wimbledon's magical Centre Court.

The Centre Court is unique in the world of tennis. Stepping out on to the perfect green grass, you immediately feel its special atmosphere. Not only is it a great place to play, but it has a sense of tradition and history that no other court in the world can match. You are aware that all the great players in tennis have played there. I still recall my excitement in 1998 when I received Wimbledon's junior trophy in the Royal Box in front of the Centre Court crowd. I knew at once that is where I wanted to play!

The Centre Court has been very special to me. Many of my happiest memories in tennis so far have come from matches there. Not only did I win my first Grand Slam title on the Centre Court at Wimbledon in 2003 but last year I was also able to win my 15th Grand Slam title which eclipsed the previous all-time Grand Slam mark set by Pete Sampras. I am fortunate to have enjoyed many successes – and I have experienced some disappointments. I am proud to be part of the story of Centre Court. I certainly hope there will be more enjoyable memories still to come.

The Centre Court entered a new era in 2009 with its sliding roof. The mix of tradition and innovation is on display for the entire world to see. As we saw and expected, everything has been designed with the care and style long associated with the All England Club and in a way that still ensures the best playing conditions for the players – even in the English rain.

I am proud to be a member of the All England Club. I am very pleased to be associated with this magnificent book capturing the history and magic of my favourite tennis arena – the premier stage in tennis.

INTRODUCTION

THE CENTRE COURT at Wimbledon is one of the world's great sporting stages – and one of the most instantly recognizable. The ivy-clad frontage, the white-clothed players looking bronzed and fit, the perfectly parallel stripes on the rich green lawn, the crisp white lines, the wooden net posts, the umpire's chair on its rubber wheels, the Royal Box, the linesmen and lineswomen immaculate in their uniforms, the ball boys and ball girls at the ready, photographers and the TV cameras in their courtside pits, the court cover neatly folded away awaiting the call to action – all are familiar sights. Even to remember them sets the pulse racing.

For tennis fans worldwide, the Centre Court is the centre of the tennis universe during those two glorious weeks each year when all roads lead to Wimbledon. Millions watch on television around the globe. For those fortunate enough to be there, the intimacy of the arena, the sense of history and the drama of the action inspire an overall sense of awe and tradition. A seat on the Centre Court is one of the most prized tickets in the whole of sport. The Centre Court is the beating heart of The Championships, the spiritual home of Wimbledon.

So it has been ever since 1922 when the All England Lawn Tennis & Croquet Club, having launched the first tournament in 1877, moved The Championships from the Club's original home in Worple Road to the larger site in Church Road, just a mile or so away. A huge new arena was constructed to accommodate some 13,500 spectators, around 3,600 of them standing. Critics at the time said the new Centre Court would be a white elephant.

In 2009 perhaps the most significant change in the long history of the Centre Court was completed. The addition of a retractable roof means that play can take place on the Centre Court even in Britain's inclement weather. No longer will the players, the 15,000 spectators or the millions of television viewers worldwide have to endure the frustration of waiting for the rain to stop.

This is the story of that single court in London SW19: its construction, evolution and new roof; the milestones that have marked the Centre Court's history as the premier stage in tennis; the grass, Wimbledon's unique and beautiful asset; the great champions and memorable matches; the umpires, officials and supporting cast so vital to the tennis theatre; activities "behind the scenes" … and the fans, without whom the Centre Court would not come alive.

If the Centre Court is a sporting theatre, the players are the leading actors. The champions of Wimbledon are integral to its history and prestige. A title triumph on the Centre Court is one of sport's most memorable achievements and in this book we give special recognition to that elite group of players who have won three or more singles titles there since the move to Church Road in 1922.

The Centre Court is never more alive than during a great match. To hear the mighty roar of the crowd after a spectacular rally, followed by a sustained burst of clapping and shouts of encouragement to both players, sends a tingle down the spine. This is sporting theatre at its very best. Running through the pages that follow are, chronologically, reminders of 39 memorable matches – matches chosen, personally and subjectively, by John Barrett as holding special significance for him. Their recall is captured, as if yesterday, through newspaper reports of the time. Not all may have produced the greatest tennis (though many have) but all are occasions etched in the rich history of the Centre Court.

This is a time to reflect on that history – recognising, of course, that it is an ever continuing story. A new generation of brilliant young athletes, including Britain's Andy Murray, will be challenging over the coming years for the game's greatest honours. Many, many more dramas are destined to unfold in the theatre of the Centre Court.

We at the All England Lawn Tennis & Croquet Club are proud to tell the story of the Centre Court so far, in both words and photographs. We hope that the words are informative and that the photographs are evocative of the colour, life and spirit of this magical sporting theatre – the jewel in Wimbledon's crown.

We are grateful to Roger Federer for writing the foreword to this book. We are privileged that such a great and graceful champion of the Centre Court has contributed his words of support.

"IT'S A SHRINE AND DRIPPING WITH TRADITION"
DON BUDGE

"IT'S A VERY NOSTALGIC PLACE.
I'VE HAD A LOVE AFFAIR WITH
WIMBLEDON EVER SINCE I CAN
REMEMBER. IT STAYS WITH YOU"
FRED PERRY

"THERE ARE SO MANY WONDERFUL
MEMORIES IN THAT PLACE, IT'S
SO FULL OF INSPIRATION, THAT
CENTRE COURT"
VIRGINIA WADE

"TO BE OUT THERE ON CENTRE COURT IS THE
GREATEST FEELING IN THE WORLD"
ANDRE AGASSI

"THE CENTRE COURT IS AS GOOD AS IT GETS"
TIM HENMAN

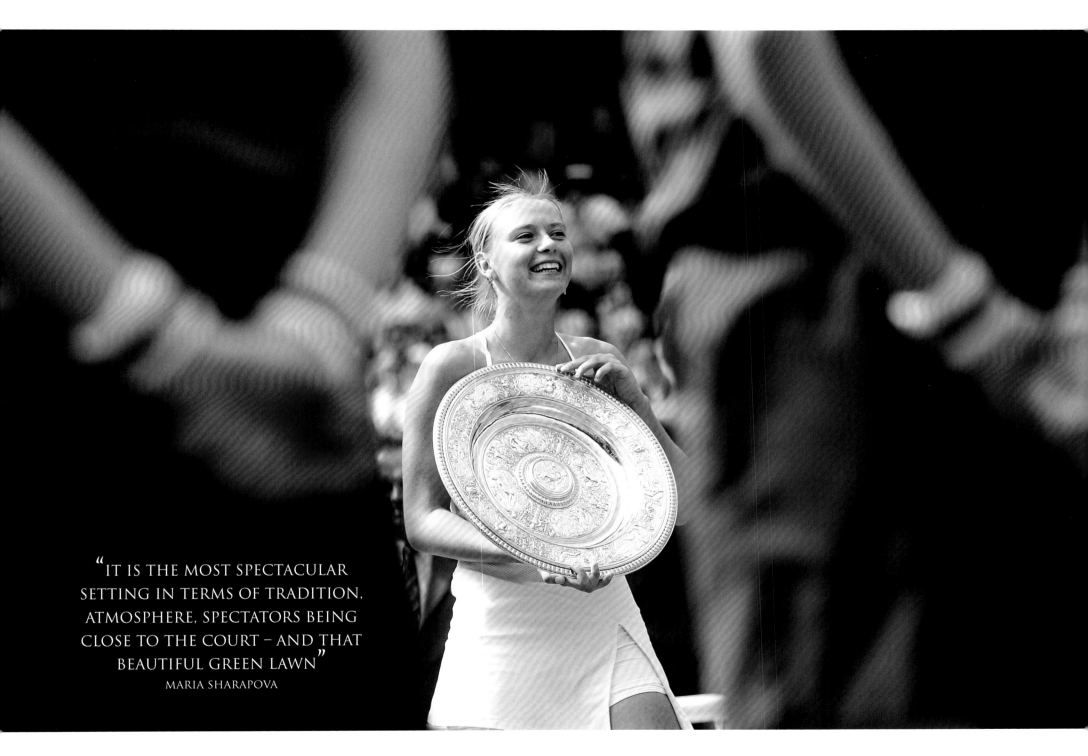

"IT IS THE MOST SPECTACULAR
SETTING IN TERMS OF TRADITION,
ATMOSPHERE, SPECTATORS BEING
CLOSE TO THE COURT – AND THAT
BEAUTIFUL GREEN LAWN"
MARIA SHARAPOVA

"THERE'S NO OTHER STAGE QUITE LIKE IT"
JOHN McENROE

"THE CENTRE COURT IS A VAST GREEN AMPHITHEATRE FILLED WITH EXCITEMENT, ANTICIPATORY SILENCES, DISAPPOINTED GROANS AND RAPTUROUS APPLAUSE – AND THEN, FOR ME, THE STAGE FOR THE REALISATION OF A DREAM"
ANN JONES

"CENTRE COURT WAS A FIELD OF DREAMS THAT I WAS ALLOWED TO SHARE WITH TENNIS LEGENDS OF THE PAST... I FELT SURROUNDED BY THE PAST, PRESENT AND FUTURE OF TENNIS"
RICHARD KRAJICEK

"THE MOST SATISFYING MOMENT IS TO WIN THE LAST POINT OF A MATCH ON THE CENTRE COURT – ESPECIALLY A FINAL AGAINST JOHN McENROE!"
BJORN BORG

"THE CENTRE COURT WAS FOR ME LIKE THE SCALA OF MILAN FOR PAVAROTTI"
ILIE NASTASE

"IT HAUNTS YOU. IT EXCITES YOU. IT CAN TAKE YOUR BREATH AWAY AND YOU FEEL ON TOP OF THE WORLD. THERE'S NO OTHER COURT LIKE WIMBLEDON'S CENTRE COURT"
MARK WOODFORDE

"THE WORLD'S ULTIMATE TENNIS STAGE"
TONY TRABERT

"JUST WALKING OUT THERE IS LIKE BEING IN A MAGIC SHOWCASE OF THE TENNIS WORLD"
JIMMY CONNORS

"THE COURT HAS SO MUCH HISTORY. IT HAS A UNIQUE FEEL ABOUT IT. I AM SURE THAT AURA WILL NOT BE LOST WHEN THE ROOF IS BUILT"
FRANK SEDGMAN

"IT WAS AT FIRST FOR ME A LONELY PLACE BUT I GREW TO LOVE THE EXPERIENCE OF WALKING OUT TO THE CHEERS OF THE CROWD. NERVOUS BUT EXHILARATED – A FEELING I STILL SENSE WHEN WATCHING TODAY'S CHAMPIONS"
ANGELA MORTIMER

"THIS IS THE SPECIAL PLACE YOU DREAMED OF PLAYING WHEN YOU WERE YOUNG, THE BIGGEST STAGE IN TENNIS"
LLEYTON HEWITT

"THERE'S STILL NO PLACE LIKE IT IN THE WORLD"
MARGARET DU PONT

"THERE'S NOTHING LIKE IT IN SPORT"
PAT CASH

"I JUST WANTED TO WIN WIMBLEDON. I WANTED TO BE PART OF HISTORY"
SERENA WILLIAMS

"THERE IS NO OTHER CENTRE COURT IN THE WORLD THAT HAS THE ATMOSPHERE OF WIMBLEDON"
ROY EMERSON

"WIMBLEDON IS MY DREAM... THAT WAS THE ONE.
THAT GAVE ME SO MUCH SELF-MOTIVATION"
RAFAEL NADAL

"I GOT GOOSE BUMPS WALKING OUT THERE THE FIRST TIME.
IT'S JUST MAJESTIC"
ANDY RODDICK

CENTRE COURT
MILESTONES

SINCE its construction and opening in 1922, the Centre Court has been the scene of countless "firsts" and sporting achievements. Here is a whistle-stop tour through time: a selection of milestones in the history of the Centre Court as a sporting theatre. The facts may be barely stated… but the milestones resonate with memory and achievement.

1922

The opening day, 26th June 1922. King George V and Queen Mary were present. Play was delayed because of rain. At 3.30pm the King appeared in the Royal Box, gave three blows on a gong and declared the new grounds open. At 3.45pm Leslie Godfree served the first ball to Algy Kingscote, who netted the return. Godfree raced forward and pocketed the ball as a memento of the historic occasion.

1922 also marked the abolition of the Challenge Round. If the previous year's singles winner wished to defend, he or she now had to "play through" by competing in the opening round along with all other players. A new era had begun.

The first singles champions on the new Centre Court were Suzanne Lenglen of France and Gerald Patterson of Australia. Suzanne Lenglen's victory over Molla Mallory, 6-2 6-0, took 23 minutes and remains the shortest ladies' singles final ever.

1923

This was the last occasion that the five Championship events were designated 'World Championships on Grass'. They reverted to their former title as 'The Lawn Tennis Championships'–known in the tennis world simply as 'The Championships'.

◄ The players arrive (top) on court for the opening match in 1922 and Leslie Godfree (bottom) serves the first ball

1924

Britain's Kitty McKane defeated Helen Wills in the ladies' singles from a set and 1-4 down. This would be Wills' only singles defeat at Wimbledon.

1925

Suzanne Lenglen won her sixth ladies' singles title. Lenglen and American Elizabeth Ryan also won their sixth ladies' doubles title together.

1926

On the opening day of the Jubilee Championships, 34 surviving singles and doubles champions (*including, previous page, Suzanne Lenglen*) were presented on the Centre Court to King George V and Queen Mary.

Britain's Leslie Godfree and Kitty Godfree (née McKane) became the first and only husband and wife pair to win the mixed doubles title.

1927

The first radio broadcast from the Centre Court took place.

American Sidney Wood, aged 15, caused a stir by playing on the Centre Court dressed in white plus-fours and golfing socks rather than the traditional flannel trousers.

Henri Cochet won the men's singles after saving six match points in the fifth set against Jean Borotra. In the semi-final Cochet had beaten Bill Tilden in five sets after being two sets and 1-5 down.

Suzanne Lenglen on her way to victory in the 1922 Championships

1930

Bill Tilden won his third singles title at the age of 37. By becoming champion nine years after his last title, Tilden set a record unequalled in the men's game.

1931

Joan Lycett became the first woman to play on the Centre Court with bare legs and ankle socks.

1933

Bunny Austin became, on the first Thursday, the first man to play on the Centre Court wearing shorts.

Jean Borotra and Jacques Brugnon, two of the four great French 'Musketeers', won their second men's doubles title together. Each had won previous titles with separate partners (Borotra with René Lacoste and Brugnon with Henri Cochet).

1934

Fred Perry and Dorothy Round won the singles titles – the first British double since 1909.

The Centre Court was the stage for Great Britain's 4-1 win over USA, inspired by

Fred Perry, in the Challenge Round of the Davis Cup held at the end of July.

1935

Helen Wills-Moody became the first ladies' champion to win after saving a match point in the final (against Helen Jacobs).

The Centre Court saw Great Britain successfully defend the Davis Cup by beating USA 5-0 in the Challenge Round.

1936

Fred Perry beat Gottfried von Cramm 6-1 6-1 6-0 in 40 minutes, the shortest men's singles final. Perry became the first player to win the men's singles three times in succession since the abolition of the Challenge Round.

Great Britain won the Davis Cup for the third successive year defeating Australia 3-2 in the Challenge Round on the Centre Court. Fred Perry beat Jack Crawford in the deciding match.

1937

On Sunday 9th May, three days before the Coronation of King George VI, an inter-denominational service of thanksgiving was held on the Centre Court.

Matches at The Championships were televised for the first time. BBC transmissions took place from the Centre Court for up to half an hour each day. On the opening day, viewers saw 25 minutes of Bunny Austin against George Lyttleton Rogers.

Don Budge became the first man to win three titles in the same year.

Great Britain's run in the Davis Cup came to an end with Fred Perry's departure to the professional ranks. USA beat them 4-1 in the Challenge Round on the Centre Court.

1938

The Wightman Cup between ladies' teams representing Great Britain and the USA was played on the Centre Court for the last time, with the USA winning 5-2. (Subsequently, the event was staged on No. 1 Court.)

Helen Wills-Moody won the ladies' singles for the eighth time, a record later broken by Martina Navratilova in 1990.

Don Budge won the men's singles and went on that year to become the first man to achieve the Grand Slam (winning the Australian, French, Wimbledon and US titles in the same calendar year).

1939

Americans won all five titles for the second year running, with Bobby Riggs and Alice Marble both becoming triple champions.

⚆ Yvon Petra of France, the last champion to wear long trousers, leaps the net to shake hands with Australia's Geoff Brown after their final in 1946

Ted Schroeder was the first champion to be presented with his trophy actually on court after the match.

1952

Frank Sedgman of Australia, having won the singles, became a three-time winner of the men's doubles.

For the first time, all eight seeds in the men's and ladies' singles reached their appointed places.

1953

America's Shirley Fry and Doris Hart won their third ladies' doubles title together.

1954

Maureen Connolly, aged 19, won the ladies' singles for the third successive year. The title formed part of her Grand Slam which she was the first woman to achieve.

Jaroslav Drobny beat Ken Rosewall 13-11 4-6 6-2 9-7 in two hours, 37 minutes, the most games then played (58) in a men's singles final. Drobny was the first left-hander to win the men's singles on the new Centre Court. He was also the first singles champion to wear glasses in the final.

Louise Brough and Margaret du Pont won their fifth ladies' doubles titles.

1940-45

The Championships were suspended during the Second World War. The military used the grounds and Clubhouse for a variety of purposes, including a decontamination unit set up under the Centre Court in case of a gas attack.

On the night of Friday, 11th October 1940 a "stick" of five 500 pound bombs straddled the Club grounds. One struck the roof of the Centre Court.

1946

The Championships resumed. Service personnel from the Army, Royal Navy and Royal Air Force were used as stewards for the first time in addition to the Honorary Stewards.

1947

Jack Kramer was the first singles champion to wear shorts.

1949

Lineswomen officiated on the Centre Court for the first time.

Bomb damage struck the Centre Court in October 1940 and resulted in the loss of around 1,200 seats for the first three meetings after the War ➤

1955

Louise Brough won her fourth ladies' singles title, not losing a set in her campaign.

1956

Lew Hoad, having won the singles, partnered Ken Rosewall for their second men's doubles title together and Hoad's third in total.

1957

Queen Elizabeth II attended The Championships for the first time. She presented Althea Gibson with her trophy for the ladies' singles on court. Althea Gibson was the first African-American to win the singles,

1962

Queen Elizabeth II attended and presented the trophy to the men's singles winner, Rod Laver, on court. It became the year of his first Grand Slam.

1963

Entry conditions for The Championships laid down for the first time that (except for a cardigan, pullover or headwear) competitors must be dressed "predominantly in white" throughout.

1964

Maria Bueno won her third ladies' singles title with victory over Margaret Smith 6-4 7-9 6-3.

◄ Queen Elizabeth II presents the ladies' trophy to Althea Gibson in 1957.
Gibson was the first African-American to win the singles

1966

Billie Jean King won her first singles title, the first ladies' champion to wear glasses in the final.

1967

The first scheduled colour television transmission in this country took place on the first Saturday, when BBC2 showed a four and a half hour programme from the Centre Court, commencing at 2pm.

The first match shown was Roger Taylor versus Cliff Drysdale.

An invitation tournament for men, the Wimbledon World Professional Championships (sponsored by the BBC to mark the introduction of colour television), was staged over three days in August. Eight 'professional' players competed on the Centre Court for prize money for the first time. Rod Laver won

the £3,000 first prize, beating Ken Rosewall in the final.

1968

Wimbledon led the rest of the tennis world by opening The Championships to professionals and amateurs alike, drawing an end to the years of 'shamateurism'.

◄ Princess Marina examines
Billie Jean's metal racket in 1968

Jimmy Connors and Arthur Ashe
during the 1975 final, the first year
chairs were provided for use at
changes of ends ➤

Rod Laver and Billie Jean King became the first singles champions of the 'open' era, winning prize money of £2,000 and £750 respectively.

Billie Jean King was the first champion to use a metal racket.

1969

The programme for the finals was changed. The finals of the ladies' singles and men's doubles were played on the Friday and the final of the men's singles was played on the Saturday along with the ladies' doubles and mixed doubles. This practice continued until Sunday play began in 1982.

Rod Laver won the men's singles for the fourth time. Laver went on to achieve the Grand Slam that year – for the second time.

Ann Jones won the ladies' singles, the first left-handed woman to do so. Princess Anne presented the winner's trophy.

1970

Margaret Court won her third ladies' singles title. She beat Billie Jean King 14-12 11-9 in two hours 28 minutes, the most games played (46) in a ladies' singles final.

1971

The tiebreak system was introduced at 8-all.

John Newcombe became a three-time singles champion with victory over Stan Smith.

In the men's doubles, Roy Emerson won his third title, this time partnering Rod Laver.

1972

A dispute between the International Lawn Tennis Federation and World Championship Tennis led to many 'contract' professionals being banned from official tournaments, preventing some leading men players competing at The Championships.

For the first time, due to rain, the men's singles final (between Stan Smith and Ilie Nastase) was played on a Sunday. Spectators were admitted free of charge.

1973

The year of the 'boycott'. Another political situation resulted in The Championships being boycotted by 80 men players, who were instructed to do so by the Association of Tennis Professionals following the

Billie Jean King won the ladies' doubles and so brought her total tally of titles to an all-time record of 20 – later equalled by Martina Navratilova in 2002.

1980

Bjorn Borg, in beating John McEnroe, became the first player to win the men's singles five times in succession since the abolition of the Challenge Round. The fourth set tiebreak (18-16 to McEnroe) is still the longest tiebreak ever on the Centre Court.

John and Tracy Austin became the first brother and sister pair to win the mixed doubles title.

On Sunday morning, 13th July, a church service to commemorate the 75th anniversary of the diocese of Southwark was held on the Centre Court. 11,000 people attended.

1981

Catherine McTavish became, on the first Tuesday, the first woman to umpire on the Centre Court.

Chris Evert won her third ladies' singles title with a victory over Hana Mandlikova.

1982

For the first time The Championships were scheduled to last 13 days and for play, including the men's singles final, to end on a Sunday.

Billie Jean King won the last of her six ladies' singles titles, beating Evonne Cawley.

1977

On the opening day of the Centenary Championships, 41 surviving singles champions paraded on the Centre Court and were presented with silver commemorative medals by the Duke and Duchess of Kent.

Queen Elizabeth II attended on the second Friday. She presented the trophy on court to the winner of the ladies' singles, Britain's Virginia Wade.

1978

Bob Hewitt and Frew McMillan won their third men's doubles title together, 11 years after their first.

1979

The tiebreak regulations were changed to operate at 6-all in any set except the final set of a match.

International Lawn Tennis Federation's suspension of the Yugoslav Nikki Pilic.

Billie Jean King and Rosie Casals won their fifth ladies' doubles together.

1974

John Newcombe and Tony Roche won their fifth men's doubles title together. Jimmy Connors, in defeating Ken Rosewall, was the first men's singles champion to use a metal racket. Rosewall had reached the singles final a record 18 years after his first.

1975

Chairs were provided for the first time on court to enable players to rest when changing ends.

1984

The Ladies' Championship Centenary. On the second
Monday, 17 past ladies' singles champions were presented
on the Centre Court with a commemorative Waterford
crystal vase by the Duke and Duchess of Kent.

For the first time all five Championship titles were
retained by the previous year's winners.

John McEnroe won his third men's singles title with
victory over Jimmy Connors. In the men's doubles,
John McEnroe and Peter Fleming won their fourth
title together.

Georgina Clark became the first woman to umpire a
final on the Centre Court.

1985

Boris Becker, at the age of 17 years 227 days, became
the youngest player, the first unseeded player and the
first German to win the men's singles.

1986

At the 100th Championship meeting, yellow tennis
balls were used for the first time.

Martina Navratilova and Pam Shriver won their fifth
ladies' doubles title together. Navratilova had won
previous doubles titles with Chris Evert and Billie
Jean King.

1988

For the first time ever, no player at The
Championships used a wooden racket.

1989

Boris Becker won his third men's singles title,
beating Stefan Edberg.

1990

Martina Navratilova won the ladies' singles to achieve
the all-time record of nine victories in the event.

1991

A 'speed of service' radar gun was used for the first
time but the speeds were not shown visually on the
Centre Court.

Play took place on the middle Sunday for the first
time – due to rain in the first week. 11,000 Centre
Court tickets were available on a first come basis.

1992

In the Royal Box, on the first Monday, the Duchess

of Kent accompanied by the Duke of Kent presented a silver salver to Dan Maskell, on behalf of the Club and the LTA, to mark his retirement from broadcasting.

1993

The 100th Ladies' Championships. Surviving ladies' singles champions were presented with a special gold bracelet.

On the first Saturday, a number of the Royal Box guests were introduced to the public, including the 1933-1936 British Davis Cup team (Raymond Tuckey, Harold Lee, Pat Hughes, Bunny Austin and Fred Perry).

1994

On the opening day, the Duke of Kent presented a Waterford crystal vase to Rod Laver to mark the 25th anniversary of his second Grand Slam in 1969.

The courtside temperature peaked at a baking hot 116°F on the Centre Court during the final day.

1995

The entry condition concerning competitors being dressed predominantly in white throughout was clarified to state "almost entirely in white".

The practice commenced whereby, after the match, umpires of the men's and ladies' singles finals were presented with medals on the Centre Court.

1996

Steffi Graf won her seventh, and last, ladies' singles title with a victory over Arantxa Sanchez Vicario.

1997

By winning the ladies' singles title, Martina Hingis became the youngest singles champion this century at the age of 16 years 278 days.

Gigi Fernandez and Natasha Zvereva won their fourth ladies' doubles title together.

1998

The Duke of Kent presented a Waterford crystal vase to Don Budge to mark the 60th anniversary of his Grand Slam in 1938.

1999

Spectators were able, for the first time, to see displays showing the speed of players' services.

All five finals, due to a backlog of matches, were decided on the final day for the first time ever.

2000

The Millennium Championships. All singles' champions, doubles champions four or more times and singles finalists at least twice were invited to The Championships. The highlight was the parade on the first Saturday when 64 players were each presented on the Centre Court with a memento by the Duchess of Gloucester, Honorary President of the LTA.

A new practice was introduced for the coin tossing ceremony preceding the men's and ladies' singles final. Two youngsters, representing charities chosen by distinguished people associated with the game, tossed the coin to decide which player served first.

Todd Woodbridge and Mark Woodforde of Australia won the men's doubles for a record sixth time.

Venus and Serena Williams became the first sisters to win the ladies' doubles and the first pair to win a title as "wild cards".

Immediately after play, the BBC (Sue Barker) interviewed both singles finalists on court for the first time.

Pete Sampras won the men's singles for the seventh time, a record since the abolition of the Challenge Round in 1922.

2001

For the first time, 32 players were seeded in the men's and ladies' singles events.

The scheduled start of play on the Centre Court was changed to 1pm on the first 11 days, with both final days starting still at 2pm.

Goran Ivanisevic became the first "wild card" to win the men's singles title.

2002

For the second time ever, two sisters (Serena and Venus Williams) contested the ladies' singles final and as a pair won the ladies' doubles title for the second time as 'wild cards'.

2004

Before play on the first Saturday, the London stage of the torch relay for the Athens Olympics was launched. In a short ceremony in the Royal Box the torch was lit and passed to Sir Roger Bannister (the first four minute miler) who saluted the crowd before walking through the Clubhouse to pass the torch to Tim Henman who later passed it to Virginia Wade.

Todd Woodbridge and Jonas Bjorkman won their third men's doubles title together. For Woodbridge, it was a record ninth title.

2005

After the men's singles final, the Duke of Kent presented Waterford crystal vases to Alan Mills (Referee) and Christopher Gorringe (Assistant Secretary/Secretary/Chief Executive) in recognition of their retirement after 23 and 33 years respectively.

2007

Equal prize money was awarded for the first time to men and ladies in all events.

The Hawk-Eye electronic line-calling system was used for the first time.

2008

Rafael Nadal defeated Roger Federer 6-4 6-4 6-7 6-7 9-7 over four hours, 48 minutes of play – the longest ever men's singles final and, with the match heavily disrupted by rain, the latest ever finish at 9.16pm.

2009

On 17th May, a special event - *A Centre Court Celebration* - was held to test the new roof and the air management system with live tennis, but also with musical entertainment, before a capacity crowd.

The retractable roof was used for the first time in The Championships. On the second Monday rain interrupted the second set of the ladies' fourth round match between Dinara Safina and Amelie Mauresmo. Mauresmo served the first ball under the closed roof but it was Safina who won the point and eventually won the match in three sets.

Serena Williams took the ladies' title for the third time with a 7-6 6-2 win against her sister Venus who had also been her final opponent in her two previous

successes in 2002 and 2003
to win a fourth doubles titl

Roger Federer won the me
sixth time. This was also his
success, a total that surpasse
shared with Pete Sampras fo
Open victory one month e
American was among the g
to witness the occasion, alo
champions, Rod Laver and
defeated Andy Roddick 5-
third victory over the Ame
final. The match lasted four
The 77 games were the mo
Wimbledon and the fifth s
played in the title round.

KITTY McKANE d. HELEN WILLS

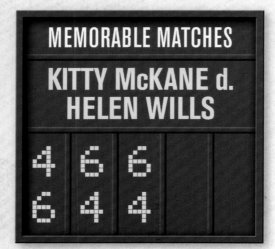

4	6	6	
6	4	4	

When the new US champion, 18-year-old Helen Wills, arrived at her first Wimbledon in 1924 she had already won the hearts of her countrymen. She was regarded by many as a future superstar. Some even thought she might dethrone the reigning five-time champion, Suzanne Lenglen. Wills duly arrived in the final but Lenglen had retired from Wimbledon at the semi-final when she became ill. Britain's Kitty McKane, now 28 and the beaten finalist in 1923, had a second chance to fulfil a lifetime's ambition.

SPECTACULAR RECOVERY GIVES BRITAIN A FIRST POST-WAR CHAMPION

Lawn Tennis and Badminton
12th July 1924
By John Dorey

Miss McKane survived the semi-final round with a walk-over from the champion, and thus came upon Miss Wills in the final. The Englishwoman's recovery from a seemingly hopeless position in the second set of the final against the American was altogether admirable.

For a moment Miss Wills had apparently reached an impregnable redoubt. England's first line trenches gone, the second line pierced and the 'enemy' swarming through – in other words America 6-4, 4-1 and a point for 5-1. During the middle part of the match Miss Wills, carrying the score from 1-3 in the first set to 4-1 in the second and winning nine games out of the eleven played, dominated her opponent with wonderful driving, taking games to love or fifteen with fast and admirably placed returns.

Miss Wills was unquestionably the better stroke-maker. Another year or so and she will be a class ahead. Miss McKane was the better runner, much more agile at the net, and much more expert in attack on the volley.

Undeniably it was that good net play which carried Miss McKane through a close third set. It secured her the sixth game for 3-3, carried her to 5-3 in the eighth, again her service game. That Miss McKane was able to close out the match two games later speaks well of her ability to keep a steady nerve. She was not afraid to win when the greatest of prizes was in sight.

It may be well to recall that the last ladies' Championship to be won by an Englishwoman was in 1914 by Mrs. Lambert Chambers.

HENRI COCHET d. BILL TILDEN

2	4	7	6	6
6	6	5	4	3

It was the semi-final in 1927. The Frenchman, Henri Cochet, faced Bill Tilden, the great American who had not appeared at Wimbledon since his second victory in 1921. Tilden had nevertheless won six consecutive US titles, had led his country to six Davis Cup successes and was widely regarded as the greatest player who had ever lived. It became one of Wimbledon's most extraordinary comebacks.

COCHET BEATS TILDEN

DRAMATIC LAWN TENNIS

WINNER'S GREAT RECOVERY

Daily Mail
1st July 1927
By Stanley N. Doust

Never have there been such stirring scenes, such electrifying tenseness in the lawn tennis championships at Wimbledon as there were yesterday.

The great arena around the Centre Court was packed. People climbed to all kinds of places and held on all through that wonderful 5 sets match when Henri Cochet of France beat W.T. Tilden, the greatest lawn tennis player of his time by 2-6 4-6 7-5 6-4 6-3.

The match was dramatic in every sense of the word – I have never seen a more dramatic one. Fortunes changed with the suddenness of an unexpected clap of thunder.

Tilden won the first two sets and led by 5-1 in the third set and required but one more game for the match. He gained that position by crashing services and devastating drives; indeed, the speed was so great that Cochet up till then had literally been knocked off the court.

How could anyone live against such wonderful lawn tennis? Was there anyone who could beat him? At 5-2 there was not one among the thousands present who did not expect Tilden to win on his "cannon ball" service. Tilden in the next game began by serving two of those express deliveries but Cochet returned and won both of them. Then the collapse came. Why it came is a mystery. Cochet pulled up from 1-5 to 5-all, during which he won 17 points in succession. It was his wonderful steadiness, superb tactics

and perfect coolness that gave him the victory.

Having survived the third set, Cochet gained confidence with every stroke he played. Tilden led 3-2 in the fifth set but wearied. Cochet continued his clever tactics with a remorselessness that was almost heartbreaking and went out by winning four successive games to end what might be described as the greatest lawn tennis match in history.

BUILDING A SPORTING THEATRE

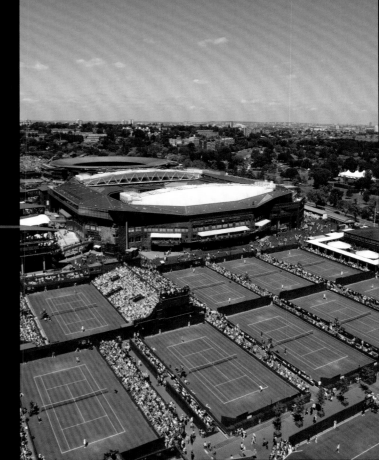

BY THE EARLY 1900s the All England Lawn Tennis & Croquet Club had outgrown its home in Worple Road, Wimbledon, where it had been since its formation (as the All England Croquet Club) in 1868. Much had changed since the first ever Lawn Tennis Championship in 1877, the final of which attracted 200 spectators. The existing Centre Court, so called because it was situated in the middle of the site with the other nine courts (or lawns as they were originally known) arranged around it, could seat only 3,500 people, was covered on only three sides and there was no room for further expansion.

So, in 1920, the decision to move was taken. A site was chosen – a meadow and farm land (*photographed overleaf in the summer of 1921*) on the other side of Wimbledon Hill, just a mile or so from the Worple Road site – and the major undertaking of designing and constructing the new Centre Court began. Although the new court would not, initially at least, be surrounded by outside courts, the inspired decision was taken to retain the name of its predecessor.

Well-known architect Captain Stanley Peach of Belgrave Road, London SW1 was commissioned to design the new Centre Court. An extraordinary character, Peach was also an adventurer, doctor and surveyor who specialised in building power stations and was a consultant on the building of many London theatres. To convince the Club's Committee, he built a huge scale model of Centre Court which "occupied the whole of a very large room". His original tracing cloths, and many of his hand-coloured elevations and blueprints, have recently been rediscovered and added to the Museum's collections. It was a vision which has stood the test of time.

A driving force throughout the project was Commander George Hillyard, Club Secretary since 1907 and once a men's doubles finalist. He collaborated with Peach on the ambitious design and his mission for the Club was clear:

> "LET US LOOK TO IT THAT WE CONSTRUCT AND EQUIP OUR GROUND THAT IT WILL IMMEDIATELY BE RECOGNISED AS THE FINEST, NOT ONLY IN ENGLAND, BUT IN THE WORLD"
> COMMANDER GEORGE HILLYARD

⋏ The former grounds at Worple Road with the "old" Centre Court

Drawing of Stanley Peach by Marion E. Knight

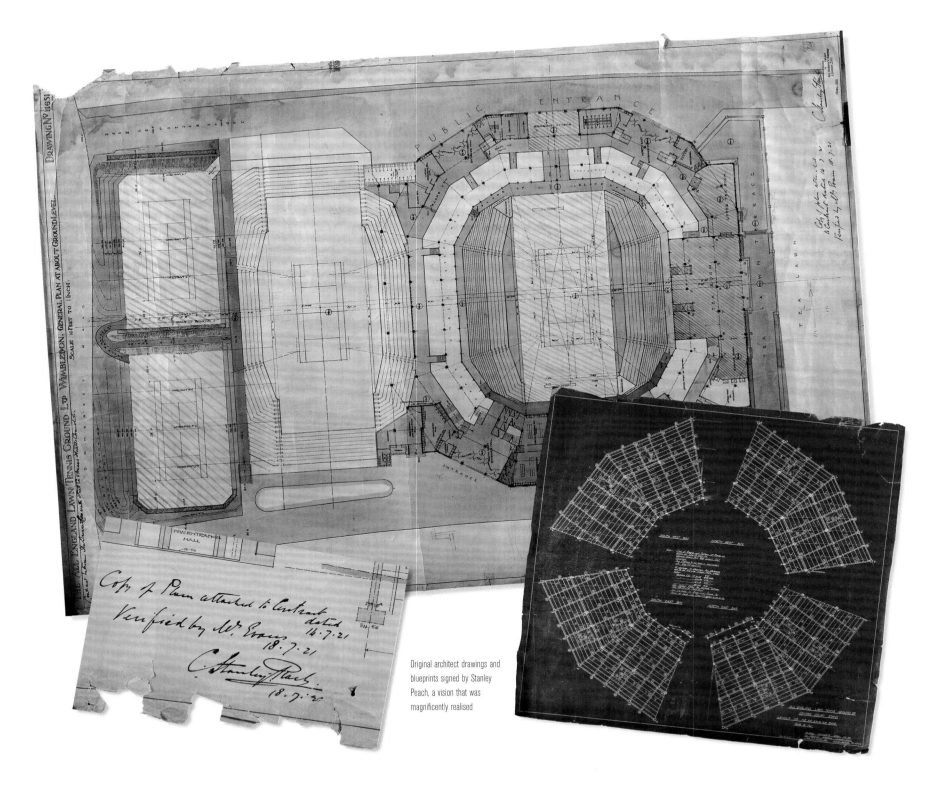

Original architect drawings and blueprints signed by Stanley Peach, a vision that was magnificently realised

THE DESIGN AND CONSTRUCTION CHALLENGE

Construction of the new Centre Court commenced on 9th September 1921. The stadium as a whole, including the court, would cover an area of nearly one acre and would be the largest re-inforced concrete structure of its day.

Some 3,000 tons of shingle, 1,700 tons of sand and 600 tons of cement were used in Centre Court's construction and nearly 21 miles of wooden slats were used for the seating. On average, there were 350 men employed on the construction project every day

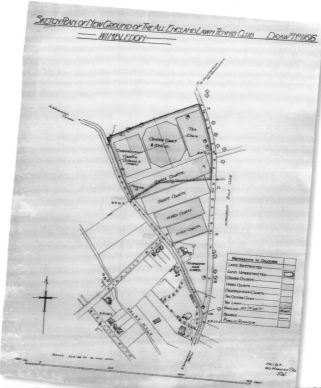

and according to British Builder they were *"not a little hampered in their work by the fact that the playing court was being prepared at the same time"*. This meant that a Scottish crane with a long radial jib *"which would have greatly facilitated the building work"* could not be erected in the middle of the site.

A Southfields' resident, then aged 10, recalls: *"One Sunday summer evening, my parents took me for a walk. We came on a building site and just walked in – all open and no hard hats in those days. We walked across a hollow. My father said, 'This is going to be the new Centre Court.'"*

⌄ Construction work in February 1922, less than five months before the opening | Sketch plans of the grounds, with the Centre Court at the top ➤

The Centre Court just six weeks before the start of the 1922 Championships ➤

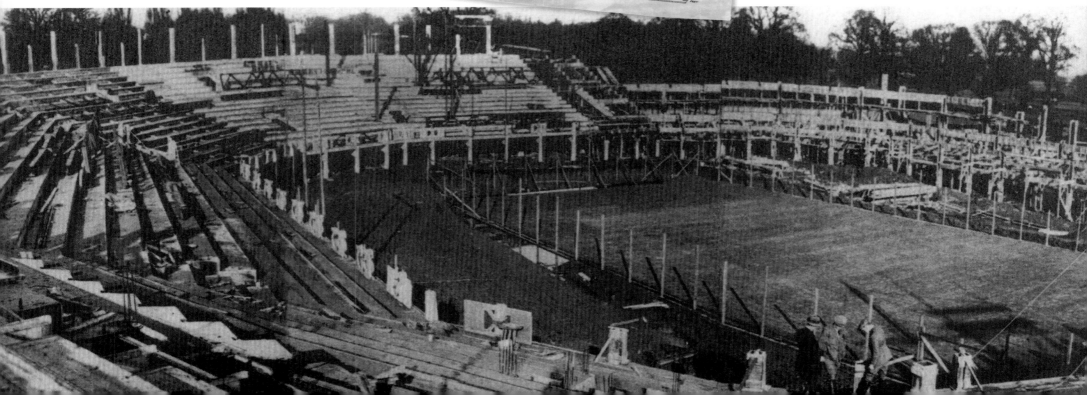

Seating capacity of the new Centre Court was 9,989 with standing room for an additional 3,600, accommodating 10,000 more spectators than the stadium at Worple Road.

Sight lines were vital. It was said that a disc of white paper, the size of a farthing in diameter, could be seen from every seat in the stand (except about 100 which were obstructed by the pillars supporting the roof). The furthest seat in the new stand was 49 yards from the centre of the court and a contemporary memorandum quaintly explained:

"*No sportsman with average eyesight has the slightest difficulty in distinguishing birds at this distance and, therefore, the general public should be able to see all the niceties of the game…*"

Everything had been planned in meticulous detail. The Centre Court was positioned very nearly on a north/south axis so that any shadow from the roof would not appear on the court itself until around 7pm.

In 1921 the groundstaff, helped by 16 labourers, began to construct and lay the grass court. The original idea for the Centre Court – for "sentimental reasons" – had been to bring the turf from the old ground to the new. But this was judged too risky with the clock ticking down to the 1922 Championships and, instead, the turfs were brought from Cumberland. Before the new grass was delivered, Commander Hillyard wrote: "*Insist that the turf is cut into foot squares, and not delivered in turfs three feet long by one foot broad, rolled up like a jam roll*".

The new Centre Court was ready – completed just in time for the 1922 Championships.

⋀ The Tea Hall under the east side of the Centre Court, seating approximately 1000 people

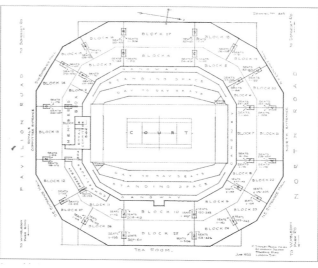

⋀ A front view of Centre Court in 1922, with workmen putting finishing touches to the paintwork

◀ Design layout of the Centre Court, with 47 different entrances

A front view in 1956 of the Centre Court with the extended balcony and with Head Groundsman, Edwin Fuller, in the foreground ➤

"THE TURF USED CAME FROM SILLOTH, A SEA-MARSH TURF. I REMEMBER IT WAS "ALIVE" WITH SOMETHING NOT UNLIKE SHRIMPS!"
EDWIN FULLER, HEAD GROUNDSMAN (1938-67)

THE CONTINUING CHANGES

Every leading venue – and especially a world-class sporting theatre - must continue to evolve to meet the expectations of its audience and leading players. The Club is constantly aware of the need to make ground improvements and provide facilities compatible with the demands of modern day sport. Changes have continued to be made to the Centre Court building over the decades since 1922 – but without losing the essential features of Stanley Peach's original structure. Each year observers will note changes… none more so than in 2009.

The Centre Court surface was completely relaid in 1926 with turf taken from two outside courts. Three years later, two electric scoreboards were installed to replace the two manually operated scoreboards (then on each side of the court rather than at the ends). These were, in turn, replaced in 1930 with larger displays, which also showed previous sets and games. Two electric clocks were fitted in the Centre Court and one large clock fitted over the main entrance of the Club.

The 1950s saw the construction, in 1955, of the now familiar balcony over the main entrance to the Clubhouse. The whole of the Centre Court structure was re-cemented, waterproofed and re-sprayed green. This involved the Boston Ivy creeper (Stanley Peach's original idea) being held back on special scaffolding away from the walls while the work was in progress. Over 3,500 nails were used to secure the creeper. In the same year, all the seats in the Centre Court were modified by the provision of curved, plastic back-rests. The wooden sight screens at each end of the Centre Court were rebuilt in concrete.

◄ (top) The Centre Court in 1922 with room for 1800 standing spectators on each side of the court and a seating capacity of 9,899

◄ (middle) The east side of Centre Court in with the original grassed Tea Lawn and a flower bed in the foreground

◄ Wooden benches being laid on the Centre Court in the early days - before individual seats appeared

The principal change during the 1960s was the completion, in 1967, of a new debenture holders' lounge and restaurant which was built along the east side of the Centre Court.

The Club entrance hall and staircase were redesigned in 1971. The distinctive balcony over the main entrance to the Clubhouse was doubled in width in 1975. Also in 1975, a new building on the east side was constructed above the debenture holders' lounge and restaurant. This was to house the Wimbledon Lawn Tennis Museum and Library which opened in 1977. At the end of the 1970s, the perimeter roof of the Centre Court was raised by one metre. This provided an additional 1,088 seats. Another major development in 1979 was the completion of a new building along the north side of the Centre Court which housed a new debenture holders' lounge on the first floor.

In 1985, the external building on the east side of the Centre Court was extended a further 25 feet over the tea lawn and a third floor added. This provided an extra 800 seats, additional media commentary boxes at the top of the stand, substantially increased accommodation and facilities for the press, a completely redesigned Museum, larger offices for the International Tennis Federation and new accommodation for office administrative staff.

The 1990s saw many changes, including the removal of the free standing areas (fondly remembered by many) on the east and west sides of Centre Court after new stringent safety legislation for sports grounds was introduced. The Centre Court became an all-seater stadium in 1990 with a capacity of 13,107 and smoking was prohibited in the covered stands. Photographers' pits were constructed, also in 1990, on each side of the court.

The Centre Court perimeter roof was completely replaced in 1992 by a new structure supported by four pillars instead of 26. This substantial operation allowed a perfect view from many seats which previously had a restricted view. At the end of 1996 the Centre Court's adjacent neighbour, old No. 1 Court, was demolished and the following year play began on the present No. 1 Court stadium constructed north of the Centre Court in Aorangi Park.

(top and middle) The free standing areas are removed to comply with new sports' ground legislation before the 1990 Championships ➤

(bottom) Demolition work in 2006 on the east side of the Centre Court building in preparation for major new catering and other facilities for the public and debenture holders which opened in 2008

THE LAST DECADE

The pace of change affecting the Centre Court has accelerated in the last decade, along with other significant developments around the grounds, under the Club's Long Term Plan.

Major refurbishment of the Centre Court commenced after the 2001 Championships. The entire facade of the building required grit blasting and the cutting out of defective concrete. This involved the complete removal of the Boston Ivy. Work on the complete refurbishment of the Clubhouse was concluded in 2002. The new main entrance hall incorporated two new twin dog-leg staircases. The front balcony was renewed and extended with bridge links to two new side balconies. New Boston Ivy was planted against the front wall of the Centre Court stadium.

Five head and shoulder busts, cast in bronze by the sculptor Ian Rank Broadley, were unveiled in front of the Clubhouse in 2004. These celebrate the victories of the five British ladies' singles champions who had won their titles at the Church Road ground – Kitty Godfree (1924, 1926), Dorothy Round (1934, 1937), Angela Mortimer (1961), Ann Jones (1969) and Virginia Wade (1977).

After the 2005 Championships, the east side of the Centre Court was evacuated to allow the continued implementation of the Long Term Plan. The perimeter roof was completely removed later in 2006, along with large sections of the north and east stands. Major construction activity took place on all fronts in 2007, including structural steelwork and the installation of new precast concrete terracing. An additional six rows of terracing were added at the top of the west, north and east sides. Rows on the north side, allowing for an extra 500 seats, were used for the 2007 Championships. New media facilities and commentary boxes were built at the top concourse level.

The 2007 Championships were unique. The perimeter roof was removed. The Centre Court was roofless for the first time in its history.

The modernisation of the Centre Court was substantially completed in 2008 apart from the installation of the retractable roof. The new fixed perimeter roof was in place — and reinstated Stanley Peach's original design with its 12-sided shape and inward slope. The new east building, which extended over the tea lawn by a further ten metres, was completely fitted out and provided improved catering facilities for the public and debenture holders. The six extra rows of terracing in the east, north and west stands increased the seating capacity of the Centre Court to 15,000.

In 2009 new, wider, padded seats (460mm in width) were installed throughout the Centre Court to provide greater comfort. There was also the new retractable roof… but more on that later.

◀ Three of the fine sculpted busts of Britain's post-War ladies' singles champions outside the Clubhouse

The 2007 men's singles final is played, uniquely, on a roofless Centre Court ➤

The Centre Court in 2008 as trusses for the retractable roof are put in place

▲ The prospectus for Debentures issued in 1920

◄ The Centre Court in 2002 with its enlarged central balcony and two new side balconies

HOW IS THE WORK FINANCED?

All these works and facility improvements have to be financed.

The All England Lawn Tennis Ground Limited (the Ground Company) was formed in 1920 to acquire the new ground, lay out the site and construct the stands. The Ground Company, led by the Club, has been responsible ever since for financing and carrying out all major capital projects approved by the Committee of Management of The Championships.

The primary funding for the construction in 1922, and for all subsequent capital improvements including the new retractable roof, has been achieved though the issue of securities known as Debentures. The original Debentures, issued in 1920, conferred upon the holder the right to a seat in the new Centre Court stand for a defined period. The Debentures raised £100,000. A new issue of Debentures was made in 1948 to raise money required to carry out repairs to the Club's premises, including the wartime bomb damage, and to improve the Centre Court facilities.

Debentures have continued to be issued to the public, usually every five years, as the principal source of funds required to carry out essential building works and major facility improvements. The holder acquires a right to a seat in the Centre Court during The Championships for a five-year period. A series of Debentures 2011-2015 was launched in spring 2009.

THE FUTURE?

The Club's Long-Term Plan for the grounds will continue but the Centre Court itself has now, in effect, been re-built – on the same site and within the same basic concepts laid down by Stanley Peach's original design 80-odd years previously. It stands ready now for another 75 years or more.

The aim continues to be simple: to ensure that the Centre Court remains at the very forefront of the world's leading sports stadia… and the premier stage in tennis.

JACK CRAWFORD d. ELLSWORTH VINES

4	11	6	2	6
6	9	2	6	4

Next, the 1933 men's final. Ellsworth Vines was the title holder. Up to this stage, the Californian had never lost a singles match at Wimbledon. A tremendous server with an immense power game, Vines was up against the superb driving control of Australia's Jack Crawford who had arrived at Wimbledon as the champion of Australia and France. The beauty, tension and excitement of the final became a Wimbledon legend.

TITLE RETURNS TO EMPIRE AFTER EPIC MATCH

The Daily Telegraph

8th July 1933

By A. Wallis Myers

Jack Crawford has made history for Australia and Wimbledon, bringing glory to both; and Ellsworth Vines helped to provide the epoch.

The final yielded one of the finest matches in the 53-year story of the Championship. There have only been ten five-set finals in the history of the meeting. Yesterday's, for superlative play,

refined co-ordination of strokes and tactics, continuous speed in service and the fighting vigour of both men at the finish, must rank first.

The match began, as all long distance journeys must, on a jog-trot note. Vines was the first to accelerate. His drives made the chalk fly in the deep corners. Vines drew first blood at 6-4.

The second set was an epic one of twenty games. It was much more than a service duel. Its facets were many, the sparkle of genius always there. At the beginning of the third set, Crawford

rolled up the sleeve of his right arm another inch. It was a signal to his friends that he meant business. In the fourth set it was Crawford who eased down. Was he keeping back his reserves for the culminating tussle which he saw was coming?

The fifth set opened with tension high. Players and crowd alike were keyed up. While play was in progress you could only hear the ping of the ball. Rarely have two valiant men given more value to a gallery.

The tenth and last game of the fifth set saw Crawford inspired and Vines his

hapless victim. We all strained forward at the first match ball. None other was required. Vines netted and the Centre Court echoed with a hundred cheers.

As the new champion and the old left the court they were saluted by more applause; as they passed under the archway which led to the dressing room both were still as self-possessed as if the match was about to begin. Australians flocked around their hero; many Americans added their congratulations. The match could have had no more sporting finish.

It was the women's final, Britain's Dorothy Round against the reigning US champion Helen Jacobs. The previous day the charismatic Fred Perry had won his first Wimbledon title amid scenes of wild rejoicing for a first British male winner since 1909. Could the Worcestershire Sunday school teacher do what Kitty Godfree had done ten years earlier and make it another success for Britain?

MISS ROUND MAKES ENGLAND'S TRIUMPH SUPREME

WOMEN'S TITLE CAPTURED - GREAT DISPLAY BAFFLES MISS JACOBS

The Sunday Times
8th July 1934
By Hamilton Price

Graced by the presence of the King and Queen, every nook and cranny was filled in the Centre Court when Miss D. E. Round of Dudley and Miss Helen Jacobs, the American women's champion, stepped on to a sun-baked court to oppose one another for the Blue Riband of women's tennis.

Miss Round became the new champion as she conquered Miss Jacobs 6-2 5-7 6-3 after a really magnificent match. The modern Wimbledon imposes on the victors what is a severe trial of strength, character and intellect and all these qualities are, happily, possessed by the quiet Worcestershire girl.

Such control of a ball minus stitches must have surprised many people; it was almost uncanny at times and the stamina of both girls was something to be admired for they had to travel several miles beneath a broiling sun.

Miss Round kept a superb length in the first set which kept Miss Jacobs more or less tucked up and caused her several times to half-hit the ball on her forehand. The reason why Miss Jacobs appeared to be playing below par was simply that Miss Round would not allow her to play otherwise, but Miss Jacobs has always been a great match-player and it was her grit and determination which enabled her to win the next set.

In the final set Miss Jacobs for once discovered that her forehand drives, loaded with 'chop', had no terrors for her opponent who brought off some beautiful crosscourt forehand drives which brooked no reply even from such a relentless retriever as the American. It was the clever and skilful fashion in which Miss Round undermined the 'chop' that helped her to gain the upper hand and when a sequence of three games fell to her in the last set a thunderous burst of applause greeted our new champion from an excited throng of spectators who were nearly leaping for joy.

GREAT CHAMPIONS

THE FIRST 50 YEARS

SUZANNE LENGLEN | 1919, 1920, 1921, 1922, 1923, 1925

I T WAS entirely fitting that the great Suzanne Lenglen, reigning Wimbledon champion and one of the greatest woman players of all time, should be the first ladies' singles winner on the new Centre Court in 1922.

Suzanne, pride of France, first came to Wimbledon in 1919 with a reputation that had been built before the four blank years of World War I. New to grass, she won a memorable Challenge Round against the holder, Dorothea Lambert Chambers, 10-8 4-6 9-7 after saving two match points. Watched by George V and Queen Mary, she unlocked the door to her unique career.

Thereafter she was never beaten in a singles that went the full distance. Suzanne was at Wimbledon from 1919 to 1926. Only in 1924 did she again lose a set, this to Elizabeth Ryan in the quarter-finals; she was ill and afterwards retired. With Ryan she had a doubles partnership that was equally flawless.

With her sparkling Gallic personality, her daringly short skirts, her balletic leaps about the court and her awesome capacity to control the ball within an inch or two, she became a legend. Crowds flocked to see her. There were few doubts that the expensive move of the All England Tennis Club from Worple Road to its new site in Church Road in 1922 would be justified.

Her subsequent final victims were Britain's Kitty McKane (1923) and Joan Fry (1925). Her superiority over all rivals grew more overwhelming. It reached a climax in 1925 when in her five rounds of singles Suzanne yielded a total of just five games. She was triple champion that year, as in 1920 and 1922.

Wimbledon in 1926 was traumatic for Suzanne. There was an unfortunate misunderstanding about the time she should play. The Centre Court crowd were incensed that their former idol had apparently been discourteous to Queen Mary who had come to watch. Suzanne stormed out of Wimbledon and never came back to the amateur game.

Her father was her mentor and trainer throughout. After turning professional, she toured for a time and later opened a lawn tennis school in France. She died an early death from leukaemia in 1938, aged 39.

Suzanne Lenglen was a champion without peer.

◄ Suzanne Lenglen during a doubles match in 1924 - note the scoreboard on the side of the court

Suzanne Lenglen's daringly short skirts set a new fashion in the 1920s ➤

BILL TILDEN | 1920, 1921, 1930

OUR NEXT champion is the peerless American, Bill Tilden. Considered by his contemporaries to have been the greatest player who ever lived, he won his third title on the new Centre Court in 1930 – straddling the move to the new ground since he had won the last two Championships played at Wimbledon's original Worple Road ground in 1920 and 1921. 'Big Bill' was the first American to win the Wimbledon men's singles.

In an amateur age when travel to Europe meant spending a week on board an ocean liner, Tilden did not defend at Wimbledon in 1922 and did not cross the Atlantic again until 1927. Aged 34, Tilden reached the semi-finals where he lost to Henri Cochet, one of the French 'Musketeers', after leading by two sets to love and 5-1. Tilden failed again in 1928, once more at the semi-final stage, but this time to Lacoste.

◄ Bill Tilden in action in 1929

◄ Bill Tilden in full flow was an intimidating opponent

Then in 1929 he fell again to Cochet, for the third time in a semi-final.

So when he came back in 1930, now 37 years old, his chances did not appear good. Yet again he met a Frenchman in the semi-finals, Jean Borotra. Tilden cleared this hurdle by the dramatic score of 0-6 6-4 4-6 6-0 7-5 and beat his compatriot Wilmer Allison in the final. It was Tilden's farewell to the Championships. He had first come in glory to Worple Road in 1920 and he left the new Centre Court in Church Road in glory ten years later.

With a cannonball service and a rich all-round game, Bill Tilden was also a master of spin and a shrewd tactician. His world ranking was no. 1 for six successive years: 1920 to 1925. He won the US title seven times and won 13 successive Challenge Round singles in leading his country to six Davis Cup successes. He turned professional in December 1930. His flair and personality took the professional game to new frontiers.

He is remembered as one of the game's immortals.

HELEN WILLS-MOODY | 1927, 1928, 1929, 1930, 1932, 1933, 1935, 1938

FOR OVER 50 years Helen Wills-Moody's record of winning eight Wimbledon singles stood alone. She lost only at her first attempt in 1924 when, aged 18, she was beaten by Britain's Kitty McKane after winning the first set and leading 4-1 in the second. She won when she returned in 1927, beating Spain's Lilli de Alvarez in the final and she carried on winning every time she came back, the last time in 1938 when she was 32.

On the court she was as efficient as a machine with a depth and pace of drive that was never broken down. Her groundstrokes were trenchantly powerful and perfectly controlled. She never showed emotion. Her soubriquet was 'Poker-Faced Helen' and nothing could have been more apt. She was almost, but not quite, as invincible as Suzanne Lenglen, whom she succeeded as queen of lawn tennis.

During a period of seven years she

◄ Helen Wills-Moody in action during the 1933 final

won Wimbledon six times, the US title four times and the French Championships also four times. Helen did not lose a single set in singles from round two in June 1927 until the Wimbledon final of 1933. In 1932 her toughest match was a 6-3 6-1 win in the final against Helen Jacobs. In 1933 she was pressed to win the final by 6-4 6-8 6-3 against the patriotic surge of Dorothy Round.

Her next year at Wimbledon, 1935, was momentous. The final brought Helen Jacobs, a neighbour of Helen Wills-Moody in Berkeley, to within a point of winning but Wills-Moody survived to win 6-3 3-6 7-5. She did not come back to Wimbledon for another three years. She had some long sets but her eighth title in 1938 was not her most difficult; she beat Helen Jacobs 6-4 6-4 in the final.

For more than a decade Helen Wills-Moody set a standard that her rivals could only at best approach, never equal.

◄ Helen Wills (right) with Suzanne Lenglen (left) in Cannes in 1926, the only time these great champions played each other

FRED PERRY | 1934, 1935, 1936

EVER SINCE he had made himself the world table-tennis champion as a 20-year-old in 1929 Fred Perry, the son of a Labour MP, had set his sights on becoming as dominant on the larger stage. He had been playing the game for only seven years when in 1934, aged 25, he won the first of his three consecutive singles titles at Wimbledon.

Perry's first major tennis success came in 1933. His inspirational play brought Great Britain to its first triumph in the Davis Cup for 21 years. The British team having defeated Australia and the USA. Invincible in singles, Perry led his country to victory against France. At Forest Hills, he swept through the field to win the US singles title with victory over Jack Crawford, denying the Australian the first Grand Slam. Perry later became the first man to win all four major titles, though not in the same year.

Perry won his first Wimbledon singles title in 1934, beating Crawford, the holder, in three sets in the final. The next year, he mastered the German Baron Gottfried von Cramm in the final in three sets.

> **"MY GREAT LOVE AFFAIR WITH CENTRE COURT NEVER FALTERED"**
> FRED PERRY

In 1936 Perry beat Don Budge, just verging on his greatness, in the semi-finals. In the final, the last singles Perry played in The Championships, he again beat von Cramm in straight sets, although this time the German hurt his ankle in the opening game.

A little later in 1936, the Centre Court saw Perry in Davis Cup action in the Challenge Round against Australia. His invincibility was never threatened. His cunning forehand, taken on the rise and sweeping the ball deep to the corners so that he could advance to the net, had become his lethal weapon. There never was a more effectively forceful British player. At Wimbledon, he had taken three successive titles and won 21 consecutive singles. The record stood until a bright young Swede, Björn Borg, arrived on the scene in the 1970s and Perry was the first to congratulate him.

Perry turned professional in 1936. He became an American citizen and served in the US forces in World War II. Thereafter he divided his time between the USA and Britain.

Fred Perry is still the only British man to have won the singles title at Wimbledon's Church Road ground where his statue, newly sited, is rightly prominent.

◄ Fred Perry with Bjorn Borg at the Champions Dinner in 1978

Fred Perry in action against Jack Crawford in the deciding rubber of the 1936 Davis Cup, won by Perry ➤

LOUISE BROUGH | 1948, 1949, 1950, 1955

LOUISE BROUGH has the distinction of dominating the Centre Court for three successive years more completely than any other player before or since her time.

In the three meetings in 1948, 1949 and 1950, she took part in 51 matches. She won 50 of them. On the final Saturday in 1948 she played three finals, including a singles win over Doris Hart. On the final Saturday in 1949, Louise won her singles against Margaret du Pont 10-8 1-6 10-8, her doubles with Margaret du Pont 8-6 7-5, and with John Bromwich lost the mixed 7-9 11-9 5-7. Such a day's work had never been achieved on the Centre Court before. She was on court more than five hours. In 1950 she again played in all three finals and this time won them all, including retaining her singles title with another victory over Margaret du Pont.

The indefatigable Louise played every year from 1946 to 1957, save 1953. In singles she never did worse

◁ Louise Brough is presented with the singles trophy in 1949 by the Duchess of Kent

◁ Louise Brough during her 1949 winning final against Margaret du Pont

than the quarter-finals. She won her fourth title in 1955 at the age of 32, with a final victory over Beverley Fleitz, and did not lose a set. As a doubles player she belonged inseparably with Margaret du Pont with whom she won Wimbledon five times and the US title 12 times. But in the Wimbledon context she was the stronger mixed player and took the title four times with three different partners – Tom Brown, John Bromwich (twice) and Eric Sturgess.

Louise was born in Oklahoma City. She learned her lawn tennis in Los Angeles and belonged wholeheartedly to the aggressive, hard volleying Californian school. She must rank among the all-time greats of the game.

> "TO COMPETE ON THAT MOST PERFECT PLAYING FIELD WAS THE THRILL OF MY LIFETIME"
> LOUISE BROUGH

MAUREEN CONNOLLY | 1952, 1953, 1954

MAUREEN CONNOLLY was, in the history of lawn tennis, one of the very few players who stand out because they were invincible or nearly so.

The Californian's career was sadly brief, not because of illness but because she broke her leg while riding. When she did so, in 1954, she was not yet 20. As a 19-year old, she had already won the Wimbledon singles three times, the US title three times, the French twice and the Australian once. In her international career she lost just four matches, and at no time in a vital contest.

Nor had she, when she had to give up her career, fully developed as a player. Her remorseless invincibility was founded on the traditional accuracy and pace of her groundstrokes. Her backhand was probably the most punishing ever possessed by a woman. But her volleying, which had been virtually non-existent at the start, was still developing.

Maureen broke through to the top of the women's game when, at the age of 16, she won the US singles at Forest Hills. That was 1951. Her Wimbledon progress began in 1952, her first year, when she was 17. On the eve of the tournament, she developed a sore shoulder. Her coach and mentor, Eleanor 'Teach' Tennant, advised withdrawal. The inexperienced Maureen promptly dismissed her. The justification of her decision not to coddle herself was made apparent. Maureen went through the singles, not without scars,

but with assured superiority in every round. In the final, Maureen defeated the great Louise Brough 7-5 6-3.

In the 1953 final Doris Hart stretched her to her full capacity (the score was 8-6 7-5) but the likelihood of defeat on the Centre Court never loomed. 1953 was Maureen's most spectacular year. She won the Grand Slam, the first woman to hold all four major titles in the same year. In 1954, she retained her Wimbledon title with victory over Louise Brough 6-2 7-5. The peerless Maureen lost only two sets in the

⋏ Maureen Connolly is presented with the singles trophy in 1953 by the Duchess of Kent in the Royal Box

Maureen Connolly in action on the Centre Court where she was never beaten ➤

singles in her three-year reign.

Her riding accident happened immediately after winning the US clay court title in 1954 and she was unable to defend her US crown. She became a professional coach and married Norman Brinker. She died aged 34 in Dallas in 1969, a victim of cancer, leaving two young children – so young to die just as she had been so young to achieve so much.

MARIA BUENO | 1959, 1960, 1964

MARIA BUENO, from São Paulo, has been the only Brazilian woman to fill a role at the very top level of lawn tennis. That her resounding success inspired her compatriots to issue a postage stamp bearing her portrait was hardly to be wondered at. The majestic grace of her game, its fluidity, its economy of effort and its all-round effectiveness brought admiration from beyond the confines of the sport.

Maria established her championship status at Wimbledon in 1959, at her second attempt and when only 19. She played with growing confidence and lost no set in the last three rounds, defeating Darlene Hard in the final. Having also won the US title in 1959, she had her second triumph at Wimbledon in 1960, this time losing one set only – to Christine Truman in the semi-finals – before defeating Sandra Reynolds in the final.

An attack of jaundice put her out of the game in 1961. She again found her immaculate form in 1964 when she won her third Wimbledon singles, beating Margaret Smith in a high-quality final,

> "THE CENTRE COURT IS A LIVING, BREATHING, CONSTANTLY RENEWING MEMORY BANK FOR BOTH PLAYERS AND SPECTATORS"
>
> MARIA BUENO

winning 6-4 7-9 6-3. The following year Maria beat Billie Jean Moffitt in three sets in the semi-finals and again played the Australian for the title. The women's game had produced a rare trinity of excellence. This time, Margaret Smith had her revenge to win her own second title.

In 1966 Maria reached her third successive final, her fifth in all: Billie Jean King (as Miss Moffitt now was) the victor by 6-3 3-6 6-1. The year 1966 also saw the last of Maria's doubles triumphs, this time with Nancy Richey. It was her fifth. Since 1958 she had won with Althea Gibson, twice with Darlene Hard and also with Billie Jean Moffitt.

The artistry of Maria Bueno's style, marked by impeccable timing of ball and racket string, never ceased to entrance, especially in the setting of the Centre Court.

◄ Maria Bueno surrounded by photographers after her singles victory over Darlene Hard in 1959

The graceful Brazilian, Maria Bueno, was a Centre Court favourite ➤

ROD LAVER | 1961, 1962, 1968, 1969

THE HOLY GRAIL for tennis players is to win all four of the world's major Championships in the same calendar year – the Grand Slam. Only two men and four women have achieved this feat. Yet, astonishingly, one man has done it twice.

It was in 1962, just before turning professional, that Rod Laver, the left-handed Australian from Rockhampton, first matched Don Budge's feat of 1938. He did it again in 1969, in the second year of open tennis. How many titles would he have won if open tennis had come earlier?

It was in 1961 that the Queenslander had first become the singles champion at Wimbledon by containing the ebullient American Chuck McKinley in straight sets. A year earlier he had lost in the final to his fellow Australian, Neale Fraser, another left-hander. Laver's next defeat in the singles was not until 1970 when Britain's Roger Taylor beat him in the fourth round. By then, Laver was 31 years old and had won four titles and 31 consecutive matches on Wimbledon's turf. In 1962 he beat fellow countryman Martin Mulligan to claim a second title. Laver decided this was the perfect moment to turn professional to test his skills against the likes of Sedgman, Kramer, Trabert, Rosewall and Gonzales.

In 1968, when he emerged from the shadows of the professional world to win the first two open Wimbledons, Rod Laver reminded the world just what it had been missing during those six dark years. The 6-3 6-4 6-2 win over fellow Aussie left-hander Tony Roche in the Wimbledon final of 1968 confirmed his status as the world's greatest attacking player. The 1969 final win in four sets against John Newcombe was majestic in its authority. The cloak of invincibility still hung from his shoulders. It was, for Laver, his fourth consecutive singles title at Wimbledon.

With the emergence of Laver at the summit, tennis lovers were treated to a rare blend of skill, courage and confidence. His ability to hit the ball early with either slice or topspin on his single-handed backhand set the pattern for others to follow. Quick of mind and movement, Laver was the complete package: a brilliant genius and a delight to watch.

He ranks emphatically among the greatest players of all time.

> "TO PLAY YOUR BEST TENNIS ON THESE SPECIAL OCCASIONS ON CENTRE COURT HAS LEFT AN INDELIBLE IMPRINT ON MY LIFE"
> ROD LAVER

◄ Rod Laver celebrates with the singles trophy in 1969, his fourth success

Rod Laver during his 1969 final against fellow Aussie John Newcombe ➤

MARGARET COURT | 1963, 1965, 1970

AUSTRALIA'S GREATEST woman player, Margaret Smith (later Court), came from a far from affluent family background on the New South Wales–Victoria border of Australia. Her first coach, who saw her playing on public courts, switched her from being a natural left-hander into right-handed orthodoxy.

Between January 1960 (when at the age of 17 she beat Maria Bueno and won the Australian title for the first time) and her eventual retirement in 1977 she achieved virtually every possible tennis feat. She won every event – singles, doubles and mixed – at all four Grand Slam championships. She achieved the Grand Slam itself in 1970 in singles. She did the same in mixed doubles in 1963. Of the Grand Slam events, she won 24 singles, 19 doubles and 19 mixed doubles – that is 62 titles in all. Her record is without equal. Her forte was all-round power. Her athleticism was a byword.

In 1963, aged 20, she broke through Wimbledon's barrier for her first title and Billie Jean Moffitt was her victim in the final. She was a triple finalist that year. In 1964 she won 12 major titles and was a triple finalist in Australia, Italy, France and Wimbledon

◄ Margaret Court's bold attacking game was highly effective on the fast grass of the Centre Court

➚ The athleticism and fitness of Margaret Court set new standards in the women's game

> **"THE ATMOSPHERE OF CENTRE COURT WAS ELECTRIFYING… ESPECIALLY WITH THE SILENCE AND PRESENCE OF THE CROWD DURING A TENSE MOMENT OF PLAY"**
>
> MARGARET COURT

(losing to Maria Bueno). The following year brought her a second singles success at Wimbledon. It was her most emphatic victory, for she lost no sets and the only advantage set was in the final against Maria Bueno. The following year she lost in the semi-finals to Billie Jean King. She played nowhere in 1967 but returned to the international arena with the introduction of open tennis in 1968. By then she was Mrs Barry Court.

Her revival as Wimbledon singles champion came in 1970. Seeded one, she played Billie Jean King. The serve-and-volley skill shown on the Centre Court by both players was awesome. In the end Margaret won by 14-12 11-9. Her swansong at Wimbledon, when the mother of a growing boy, came in 1975 when, with Marty Riessen in the mixed, she played and won her last match to climax the meeting, recording her tenth Wimbledon title.

She retired finally in 1977. In her career she competed in 289 tournaments and won 383 events in 20 different countries, a remarkable record. In 1991 Margaret was ordained and commenced a life of religious service.

She was an extraordinary champion.

BILLIE JEAN KING | 1966, 1967, 1968, 1972, 1973, 1975

BILLIE JEAN MOFFITT, an ebullient Californian aged 17 bubbling with energy, played her first match at Wimbledon in 1961. She lost her opening singles. But in doubles her potential was evident and she won the title with Karen Hantze.

At her second visit in 1962 Billie Jean was drawn in her singles opening round against Margaret Smith, the no. 1 seed. It proved a notable clash of two outstanding volleyers and Billie Jean won 1-6 6-3 7-5. It initiated a decade of rivalry. Billie Jean's first singles title came in 1966 when (now Mrs King) she won in three sets in the final against Maria Bueno, her other outstanding rival. A year later she was unbeaten in three events. She was the first triple champion since Frank Sedgman in 1952 and, among women, Doris Hart in 1951.

The first year of the open game, 1968, saw Billie Jean taking the singles for the third successive year, this time with victory over Judy Tegart in the final. Her last defeat in that event had been in the semi-finals in 1965. In 1969, Billie Jean yielded the singles to Britain's Ann Jones. In 1970, her fifth final in five years, she lost her historic clash with Mrs Court.

Billie Jean's invincibility on the Centre Court was resumed in 1973, beating Chris Evert in the singles final and winning her second triple crown. She won again in 1975 (in a sweeping 6-0 6-1 final against

◄ Billie Jean King in action during her winning final against Evonne Cawley in 1975 | ◢ Billie Jean King receives the singles trophy from the Duke of Kent in 1975

"CENTRE COURT – MY FAVOURITE PLACE IN THE WORLD"

BILLIE JEAN KING

Evonne Cawley) to take the event for the sixth time. In 1976 her best was to reach the final of the ladies' doubles. It marked 16 years in which she had never failed to play in at least one final.

Her 20th title was won in 1979, the ladies' doubles with Martina Navratilova. Aged 39 in 1983, Billie Jean still reached the singles semi-finals and kept in the mixed as far as the final (in which John Lloyd and

Wendy Turnbull beat Billie Jean and Steve Denton 6-7 7-6 7-5). It was Billie Jean's 265th match at Wimbledon and her 28th final, of which she lost only eight – an awesome record.

At her peak it was impossible to find any aspect of her game that was less than strong; her overhead was superb and she was reputed to have gone through more than one season without ever missing a smash. She played a leading part in lifting the women's professional game towards equality with the men's.

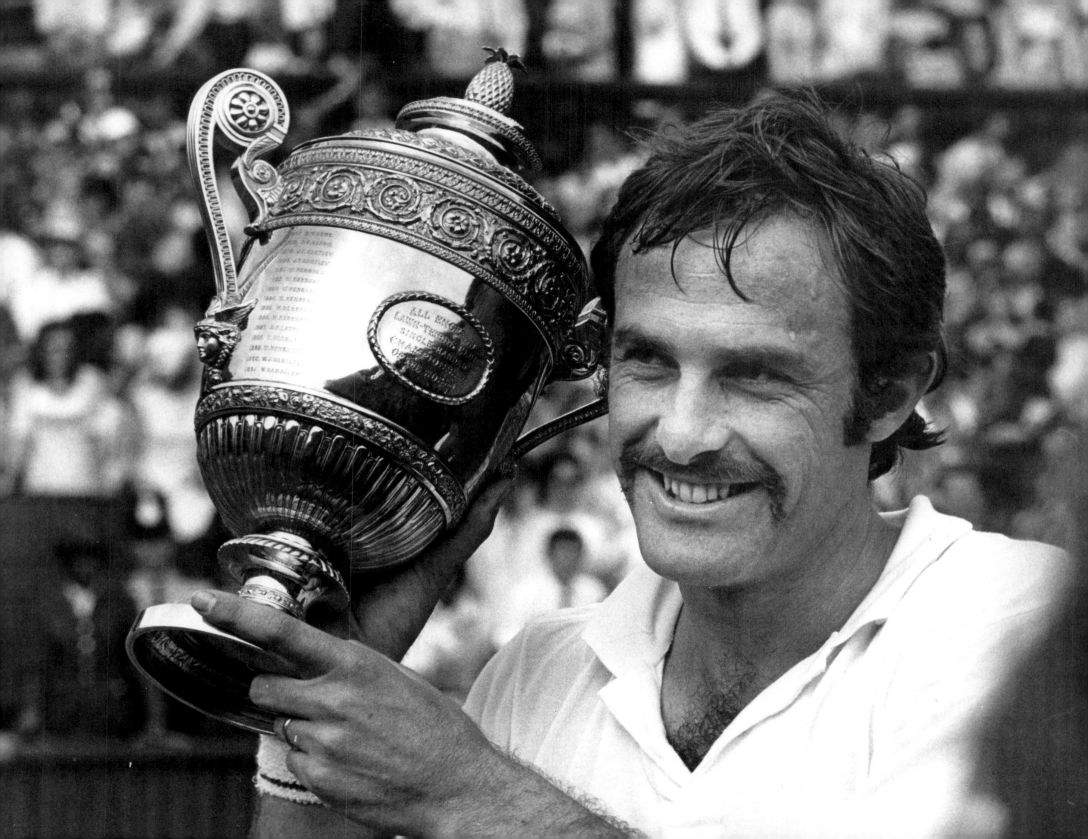

JOHN NEWCOMBE | 1967, 1970, 1971

LIKE FELLOW Australian Rod Laver, John Newcombe won the singles at both an amateur and an open Wimbledon. If tennis politics had not intruded in 1972 and 1973 when he did not play, Newcombe might also have equalled Laver's feat of winning the title four times in all.

His first Davis Cup experience was in 1963, when he was 19. He came to his peak four years later. If his progress towards greatness was slow, it was the surer for it. He was never taken beyond four sets in his first title win at Wimbledon in 1967 and the final against the unseeded German, Wilhelm Bungert, was among the easiest ever. The last 'amateur' champion, Newcombe then turned professional with Lamar Hunt's World Championship Tennis.

Arthur Ashe thwarted him in the fourth round in 1968 when he returned to an open Wimbledon. The year following, Newcombe came within one match of his second title; instead, Laver won his fourth. In 1970 he had a tremendous quarter-final tussle against Roy Emerson, surviving in the 20th game of the fifth set. He went on to win the final

against Ken Rosewall in another full-length contest. His third singles title was in 1971, again a five set final, against the American Stan Smith. Thus Newcombe made himself a three-times singles champion at his 11th appearance.

John Newcombe was one of the game's heavyweights, a resolute serve and volley man who rode out many a storm by the consistency of his attacking pressure. The French singles was the only title of consequence he did not win. A giant in singles, he was even more successful in doubles, most notably with the left-handed Tony Roche; he took five of six Wimbledon championships with him.

A doughty stalwart, Newcombe was a professional to his fingertips and one who never failed to enhance the image of lawn tennis both as a player and as a highly popular Davis Cup captain.

> "I STILL BELIEVE THE GHOSTS OF PAST CHAMPIONS RESIDE AROUND CENTRE COURT"
>
> JOHN NEWCOMBE

◁ John Newcombe celebrates victory in 1971

John Newcombe leaps the net after his first title win in 1967 against Wilhelm Bungert ▷

HELEN MOODY d. HELEN JACOBS

6	3	7	
3	6	5	

The 1935 ladies' singles final saw already six-time champion Helen Moody (formerly Wills) against Californian near neighbour Helen Jacobs. They were fierce rivals and meeting in the Wimbledon final for the third time. In the previous two matches Jacobs had won only seven games. Would this be another demolition?

MRS. MOODY REGAINS HER TITLE

EPIC STRUGGLE – MISS JACOB'S ERROR IN TACTICS

The Sunday Times
7th July 1935
By Hamilton Price

The record of seven victories in the Women's Singles Championship, held by Mrs D. K. Lambert Chambers, was equalled yesterday at Wimbledon by Mrs F. S. Moody who, on her eighth appearance in the final, beat Helen Jacobs by 6-3 3-6 7-5 after one hour and 44 minutes of some of the most tense and yet finest lawn tennis ever played by two women on the Centre Court of the All England Club.

Overnight people began to arrive outside the ground, and by eleven o'clock there was a long line of spectators stretching down the hill and up Somerset Road. There was, of course, hardly an inch to spare round the famous court, every nook and cranny filled, and the two Americans when they entered the arena met with a hearty reception.

It looked as if Mrs. Moody would triumph in two sets, but Miss Jacobs suddenly assumed a command which enabled her to win the second set at 6-3 and later establish a lead of 5-3 in the final set, and to be within a point of victory in the ninth game on Mrs Moody's service! At last it seemed that the industrious Miss Jacobs would land her reward.

That she did not was not due to any bad luck, but to the fortitude and wonderful play of Mrs Moody. There was never a loose shot from Mrs. Moody's racket, and, when once she had saved herself from what seemed impending disaster, Mrs. Moody, in the last five games, increased not only the depth but also added power to her forehand drives, thanks to the fact that, for some unknown reason, Miss Jacobs had elected to hit harder. In my opinion, this change of tactics cost Miss Jacobs a wonderful match. To Mrs Moody nothing but praise can be given.

Very few finals have been more tense and the umpire must be heartily congratulated on the admirable way he kept an excited crowd in hand. His control must have helped not a little towards such a sustained display of all that is best in the game.

Champion for the past two years, Britain's Fred Perry faced his most serious threat in the 1936 semi-final. The tall Californian Don Budge had all the hallmarks of a future champion – a fine serve, a bludgeoning backhand, great touch on the volley and the physique of a highly trained athlete. Would this be the moment when the Perry era ended or would the Englishman stay on course to become the first triple men's singles winner at the new Wimbledon?

HOLDER DEFEATS BUDGE IN FOUR SETS

The Daily Telegraph
2nd July 1936
By A. Wallis Myers

England's No. 1 took up the defence of his title against the menace from the Pacific West, the tall, loose-limbed, Vines-like Budge. They had met only twice before, Perry winning on the same court a year ago in the Davis Cup and again on the cement courts in California. In the interval Budge had forged new weapons, a steadier forehand and more refined generalship. There was never a period in a fierce four-set struggle when the challenger did not look dangerous nor require the best of Perry to beat him.

Leading 5-3, Perry's blood appeared a little hotter than was good for his cause. In his eagerness to clinch the set he overdrove the boundary and although he was three times within a point of the set his mind got ahead of his hand and a net-cord eventually squared the set. Then, favoured by fortune Budge proceeded to break through to love. His capacity for raising chalk on the sidelines was a feature of his display. In the next game he crowned his recovery by holding serve from 6-5. On the drive he was wonderfully steady and when he came to the net he had the finishing volley ready.

This initial rebuff had a stimulating effect on the champion. Now he was watching every ball and pouncing on it as if it were a panther's prey. Budge was hurled back by this retort and at 4-1 and 0-40 on the Californian's serve it seemed certain that a quick set would be placed to the champion's credit. Budge, though, was in no yielding mood and his play in the next three games drew, as deserved, the heartiest applause as he made it 4-4. But Budge spoiled his great rejoinder in the ninth game by serving two double-faults and netting a smash. He then allowed Perry to pierce his defences, losing only one point on serve, a double-fault, to level the match.

In the fourth set Budge made his last stand with becoming gallantry.

Leading 4-2 he looked really menacing. A cool and calculating hand was required at this stage and the champion supplied it. He pressed in all departments, made some amazing forehand drives on the run and some equally deadly volleys. Perry was now in full cry for home. Only three more points were sacrificed. His pressure was inexorable and his aim unfaltering.

GREEN GROWS THE GRASS

"IF TENNIS IS PLAYED WELL, IT CAN NEVER
BE MORE BEAUTIFUL THAN WHEN IT IS
PLAYED ON GRASS"
KURT NIELSEN

WIMBLEDON'S CENTRE COURT, thanks to global television coverage of The Championships, is probably the most famous piece of grass in the world. The quality of the surface is vital. Each year it must provide perfect playing conditions for the world's greatest players to display their full range of strokes.

This responsibility falls to the skill and knowledge of the head groundsman. Since 1991 Eddie Seaward, deservedly awarded the MBE in 2008 for his services to the industry, has led a team of around 15 permanent staff, augmented to twice that number with the addition of temporary staff during the period of The Championships, in undertaking this crucial task. It is a source of pride to see the great champions step onto "his" court on the first day of the third week in June every year.

"But, depending upon the weather conditions, that first day can be a nerve-wracking time," says Seaward. *"You sometimes have to make last minute adjustments. It is a great relief walking out early on the second morning knowing that all went well the day before."*

Sphairistiké **was invented by Major Walter Wingfield in the early 1870s as an outdoor game to be played on grass. It led to 'lawn tennis' as we know it. The first Championship meeting was organised in 1877 by the All England Croquet & Lawn Tennis Club (renamed that year to include the new game) and held on grass courts at the Club's ground at Worple Road in Wimbledon. Today Wimbledon is unique. Alone of the four Grand Slams, The Championships are still played on grass courts. The US Open ceased being played on grass at Forest Hills, New York in 1974 and, after three years on a US clay surface, moved to hard courts at a nearby site at Flushing Meadows. Ten years later, in 1988, the Australian Open moved from grass at the Kooyong Lawn Tennis Club to hard courts in central Melbourne. The French Championships have always been played on clay courts.**

Eddie Seaward, the Head Groundsman, in 2008 ➤

THE ANNUAL PROGRAMME OF CARE

Care of the courts is a year-round task. Annual maintenance of the Centre Court begins with a thorough soaking immediately after the end of The Championships. Renovation starts with scarifying two weeks later to remove any thatch. The court is then over-sown with perennial rye grass which, since 2000, has been used exclusively on all the courts to improve durability and strengthen the sward so that it can better withstand the increasing wear of the modern game. The use of 100 per cent perennial rye grass was the result of detailed research and testing, over a period of four years, undertaken in collaboration with the independent Sports Turf Research Institute based in Bingley, Yorkshire. (Previously the mix was 70 per cent rye/30 per cent creeping red fescue.) Finally, the court is given a light dressing of loam.

Mowing to a height of 14–16mm continues throughout the year as necessary. In December, the first of three applications of fungicide is applied. *"Now that we are using the perennial rye, it is only necessary to treat the grass three times – at the end of the year to get us through the winter, again sometime in the spring and finally shortly before The Championships when we start using the covers again."*

In the spring the court receives a shallow scarifying, using a "verticutter", before being over-sown again with grass seed. Depending upon the amount of rainfall, the court is watered to promote growth. The heavy roller, weighing one ton, is used for about half an hour to level the surface. *"It used to be rolled in the spring for between*

10 and 15 hours over a three week period," remembers Seaward. "*With the change to 100 per cent rye grass we have a more open sward which lets the air go through so the soil hardens naturally and much less rolling is required.*"

In the run-up to The Championships, the court is cut and lightly watered regularly with the cover being used if there is too much rain. The height of the cut is also gradually reduced so that by the first day it is down to 8mm. It used to be cut to 6mm, but in 1988 the Committee decided that 8mm would produce the perfect pace that was fair to volleyers and baseliners alike and it has remained at 8mm ever since. Seaward recalls that Pat Cash, who had won the singles in 1987, noticed the difference. One day the following year when Seaward passed the court where Cash was practising, he called out, "*Hey, Eddie, what have you done – it's like a jungle out here!*"

The public, too, are surprisingly alert when changes are made. "*We'd been using a new, larger mower on Centre Court and I had a phone call from someone who wanted to know why we had reduced the number of stripes between the singles sidelines from 18 to 16,*" said a smiling Seaward. "*Another year, during Jim Thorn's time, a lady had phoned to tell Jim that he had marked out the court incorrectly. On her television screen, she said, the court was much too wide at the bottom!*"

WEAR AND TEAR

In the years when men's tennis on grass was dominated by players who came in to volley behind their serves, the area of the court which experienced the greatest wear was a triangle around the "T" of the service box, with its apex about three feet up the centre line.

The invention of the lawnmower, along with pressurised rubber balls, made grass court tennis possible ➤

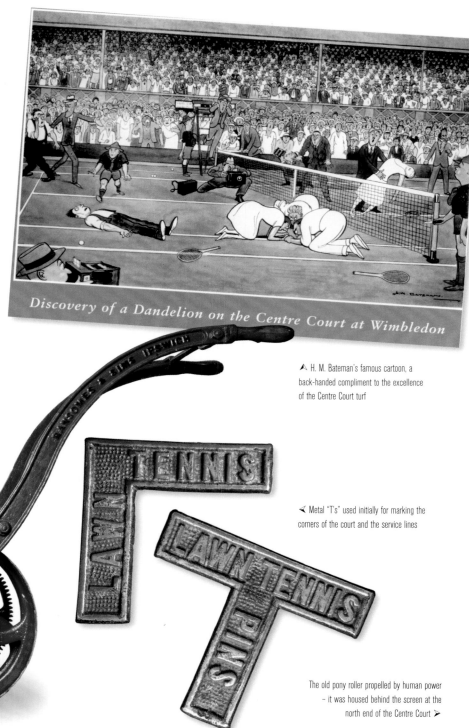

Discovery of a Dandelion on the Centre Court at Wimbledon

⋀ H. M. Bateman's famous cartoon, a back-handed compliment to the excellence of the Centre Court turf

◄ Metal "T's" used initially for marking the corners of the court and the service lines

The old pony roller propelled by human power – it was housed behind the screen at the north end of the Centre Court ➤

Over the past decade, the nature of professional tennis has changed. It is now largely a baseline duel on all surfaces, including grass, and this is now the area of the court which receives most wear.

In these areas of high activity the colour changes to brown during the course of the tournament. But the grass is not dead, merely bruised, and the bounce remains true. Watering and re-seeding quickly restores the surface. This will become crucial in 2012 when preparing the court for the London Olympics, with the tennis tournament starting just a few weeks after the conclusion of the Championships. Seaward is confident. By pre-fertilising the seed, Seaward expects his team to start mowing again ten days after the end of The Championships.

Other damage, caused by a player's racket or shoes, can be repaired overnight. *"We mix top soil with water to produce a paste which fills any gaps in the turf and then sprinkle fresh grass mowings – known in the trade as 'groundsman's paint' – onto the surface. It quickly sets hard to maintain a perfect bounce,"* explained Seaward.

But there are other hazards, including the Wimbledon foxes. Seaward recalls that *"one was very fond of sun-bathing in the afternoon on the roof of the BBC commentary box."* If a vixen urinates on the surface, *"it kills the grass stone dead and there is nothing we can do, which is why we now have a low voltage electric fence around the perimeter to keep them off. Fortunately it seems to work well."*

Roger Federer had an amusing moment one December. In *The Roger Federer Story* (2007), Rene Stauffer recounts:

"Roger Federer returned to visit the All England Club one year in December. He went into the Centre Court. 'Please don't stand on the grass,' said a stern voice over the Centre Court loudspeaker. Federer burst out laughing."

THE PRESENT COURT SURFACE

The present Centre Court grass was laid in 1997. *"The new court was my first major challenge,"* remembers Seaward. *"The old court was cambered, with a fall to each side. I wanted it flat but when we removed the turf we discovered that the ash sub-base was also*

◄ Scarifying in progress during the off-season

◄ Special lamps are now used to stimulate winter growth

cambered. So first we had to raise the sides of the sub-base to make everything level – which also meant raising the concrete surrounds – before new turf could be laid."

The turf had been ordered two years in advance from

Yorkshire. *"Soil compatibility was essential so we had shipped up tons of Surrey loam to the turf nursery,"* said Seaward. *"The seed came from Holland, in those days a mixture of rye, fescue and bent. This way we virtually eliminated a weed grass, poa annua, that had affected some of the court."*

A Championship Day in the Life of Eddie Seaward

0530	Get up and listen to weather forecast
0600	Phone the court coverers and instruct them to deflate if the forecast is good
0745	Remove the covers and instruct the team to start mowing
0800	Start to prepare for the day's play. Mow and mark every court
0900	Carry out 'Clegg hammer' bounce test on all show courts and designated outside courts
1000	Breakfast
1030	Have practice courts dressed for play
1100	Have outside courts dressed for play
1300	Have Centre Court and No.1 Court dressed for play
1400	On call throughout the remainder of the day to deal with any problems which may arise. Liaise with the Referee regarding the need to cover the courts during rainy periods and agree when play can be resumed.
2100	When play finishes, inspect each court and decide how much irrigation, if any, is required. This will depend upon the overnight weather forecast
2200	Retire to bed

Preparing, marking and testing the court during
The Championships (top & bottom) ➤

BALLS, BOUNCE AND HARDNESS

Consistency of bounce is the most important requirement for any tennis court. It is natural for all grass courts to slow down with use. As the grass loses its sap, the ball skids less and bounces higher. The height of the bounce largely depends on the hardness of the soil, not the grass. This can be controlled by watering. It can also be measured by using a device called a Clegg Hammer. This device, an impact hammer weighing half a kilo, is dropped from a height of one-third of a metre and the rebound is measured.

All tennis balls must conform to the strict specifications listed in the Rules of Tennis that govern their size, weight, compression and bounce. The last change was a minimal alteration in compression in 1995. Ever since 1902 the balls used at The Championships have been supplied by Slazenger, whose century of service was recognized in 2002 with a presentation in the Royal Box.

There have been several important innovations over the years. In 1929 hand-stitched seams gave way to vulcanised seams. Twenty-five years later a nylon-reinforced melton cloth was introduced to prolong end wear. In 1986 white balls were replaced by yellow, a colour that improved visibility for players and spectators alike, especially those millions watching on television around the world. More recently, 'day-glo' dye has been used to improve visibility still further and a wet-weather finish added to improve performance.

Balls have, since 1955, been changed for new balls after the first seven games and then after every nine games (a tiebreak counting as one game). Previously they were changed before each set. Balls are stored in a courtside

◄ Measuring soil hardness during The Championship

◄ (below) Checking ball bounce with a Cleg Hammer

◄ (far left) Balls for The Championships have been supplied by Slazenger since 1902

refrigerator on the Centre Court at 68°F and opened just before each scheduled ball change.

Paint is not used to mark the lines on the court. A transfer wheel marker is used to apply a white compound containing china clay to make it durable. All the lines are 50mm wide, except the baselines which are 100 mm.

BORIS BECKER AND MARTINA NAVRATILOVA ARE THE ONLY CHAMPIONS TO HAVE WON SINGLES TITLES AT WIMBLEDON WITH BOTH WHITE AND YELLOW BALLS

THE ROOF

Eddie Seaward relishes the opportunities provided by the new roof. Although the new perimeter roof is higher than the old one, there is now two per cent more sunlight falling on the playing area. This is important for the growth of the grass, especially at the southern end where part of the run-back area is permanently in shade.

"*I'm really excited by the whole prospect of the retractable cover,*" says Seaward. "*It is a new challenge for us and one which we welcome. It won't be long before most sports will be able to play under cover when necessary. That is the way technology is taking us. The Club conducted exhaustive tests to solve the problem of humidity and, happily, it is all working out as planned. It's great to think that Wimbledon is leading the way for grass court tennis.*"

It was the deciding rubber of the 1937 Davis Cup tie that would decide whether the United States or Germany would go through to challenge the holders, Great Britain. Donald Budge for America and Gottfried von Cramm for Germany, the two No. 1s, faced one another on the same court where just two weeks earlier Budge had secured a straight sets victory over the German in the final to claim his first Wimbledon title. As the players left the locker room, Budge recalled that von Cramm, not a Nazi supporter, received a telephone call. It was Adolf Hitler exhorting him to win for the Fatherland. Budge said von Cramm *"came out pale and serious and played as if his life depended on every point"*.

ONE OF DAVIS CUP'S GREATEST MATCHES

Ayres Lawn Tennis Almanack
1938
By A. Wallis Myers

A 1937 Davis Cup contest which America was favoured to win before a ball was struck developed into a struggle tense with uncertainty and excitement.

After two hours' play each man had won two sets, the German the first and second after a display of all-court tennis as glorious as any ever seen on the Centre Court, and Budge the third and fourth after he had recovered the range and touch that had been shaken by his adversary's marvellous aggression and sangfroid.

With splendid courage and revealing the sustained skill which had gained him mastery over the champion in the first two sets, von Cramm forced a lead of 4-1 in the final set. It brought, as it deserved, an almost overwhelming ovation from the crowd. They not only admired the winning strokes, several made from losing positions, all achieved under ruthless pressure; the German's fighting spirit had captured their hearts. And it was a lead that in almost any match except this one must have proved decisive.

The obstacle was Donald Budge and as one saw this lanky, red-haired youth, quite unperturbed by the score, quietly reduce the deficit to vanishing point one recalled that his father, a dour Scot before he emigrated to California 30 years ago, had revealed the same cool qualities in League football in Glasgow.

Amid great excitement the German took the lead at 5-4 after saving two break points. Budge retaliated by holding service to love, coming in to make three glorious volleys. But instead of the German server following suit again there is an ominous change. Budge wins von Cramm's serve in four points, storming in and smashing with deadly power.

The next was the last game but its record almost deserved to be framed in the club-house. Budge won it and with it the match after von Cramm, with superlative play, saved five match balls. No effort quite as heroic, and sustained with such gorgeous shots, had been seen at the New Wimbledon. No wonder Budge leapt over the net to shake hands with an adversary who had fought him with such superb courage.

Photographs (above and right) from the 1937 men's singles final between the same players, just two weeks before their epic Davis Cup battle

SUPPORTING CAST

THE PLAYERS are the leading actors on the stage of the Centre Court. But it would not thrive as a sporting theatre without the support of so many others. Here we recognise the role of some significant members of that vital 'supporting cast' in and around the Centre Court. It is their united contribution that helps to make Wimbledon's Centre Court the world's premier tennis stage.

CHAIR AND LINE UMPIRES

Sitting there, above the players, is the presiding figure of the chair umpire. Umpiring a match on the Centre Court is itself a great honour and responsibility… and an occasion of personal excitement for any umpire.

> "WHEN I DID MY FIRST MATCH ON CENTRE COURT I FELT SO PRIVILEGED TO BE THERE. YES, I WAS A BIT NERVOUS, YOU KNOW THE BUTTERFLIES, BUT AT THE SAME TIME I WAS VERY HAPPY. FOR ALL OF US WHO LOVE TENNIS IT IS A VERY SPECIAL PLACE."
> CARLOS RAMOS, UMPIRE (LEFT)

Around 25 officials will have the opportunity during the tournament to umpire a match on Centre Court. In total there are some 330 officials at The Championships working as chair umpires, line judges or off-court staff. Of these, around 240 are members of ABTO (Association of British Tennis Officials) including 70 who have come through the programme organised by the LTA and ABTO to encourage young people to officiate. Around 90 officials come from other countries all over the world. A team of seven ITF/Grand Slam Chair Umpires officiate at all four Grand Slams.

◀ Umpire Carlos Ramos at work on Centre Court wearing the official clothing designed by Polo Ralph Lauren

The officials are organised by the Chief Umpire who makes assignments in consultation with the Referee. The chair umpire remains the same

↖ Lineswoman Margaret Wareing keeps her eye on the ball

↖ The umpire's chair and some familiar features

throughout the match. There are nine line judges on Centre Court matches. The usual schedule is to change the line teams every 75 minutes.

Chair umpires use hand-held computers in the chair for recording the score in place of the traditional manual scorecard. This computer, which was first used in 2001, also drives the scoreboards and the point-by-point screens around the grounds. Net cord judges are no longer used at The Championships after the introduction of a net cord machine in 1991, which is operated by the chair umpire.

> "I REMEMBER THINKING, 'WOW, AM I REALLY HERE ON THE MOST FAMOUS TENNIS COURT IN THE WORLD OR IS IT A DREAM?'"
> MARGARET WAREING, LINESWOMAN (ABOVE)

BALLBOYS AND BALLGIRLS

Ballboys and ballgirls are a distinctive and well loved sight on the Centre Court.

In the 1920s and 1930s, Wimbledon's ballboys were provided by Shaftesbury Homes, the charity set up by the 7th Earl of Shaftsbury in 1843 to assist destitute children. From 1946, the youngsters were volunteers from local schools and institutions including, for over 20 years, Barnardos Homes.

Ballgirls were first introduced at Wimbledon in 1977 and in 1986 they were used on the Centre Court for the first time. The ratio of boys to girls is now approximately 50:50 and the average age is 15 years.

Local schools now supply the 250 boys and girls required for The Championships.

The successful applicants receive intensive training (often on the Club's indoor courts) from February onwards up to The Championships, directed for many years under the watchful eye of Anne Rundle. Training sessions involve general fitness and movement exercises, circuits, ball skills, scoring and "set pieces" (ball change, start and end of game, tiebreak and others).

Four teams of six are chosen to be responsible for the Centre Court and No. 1 Court during The Championships, and the competition is fierce to be selected for one of these show court teams. It is a responsible but exciting task and appearing on the Centre Court is undoubtedly an unforgettable highlight.

⌄ The attire and ages of the Wimbledon ball bays have changed over the years as these groups from the 1920s (left) and 1950s (above) clearly show

"BEING ON CENTRE COURT WAS BRILLIANT. I REALLY
ENJOYED IT, THE NOISE OF THE CROWD AND EVERYTHING ...
AN AMAZING ATMOSPHERE. TO START WITH I WAS NERVOUS
BUT YOU SOON GET USED TO IT AND IT BECAME REALLY GOOD
FUN. WHEN THE CROWD GOT GOING, I WAS REALLY EXCITED.
IT WAS BOILING HOT THAT DAY AND I FAINTED FROM
DEHYDRATION. EVERYONE WAS VERY NICE BUT I
WAS OFF COURT FOR THE REST OF THE DAY"

BALLGIRL MOLLY BISHOP (15) FROM URSULINE HIGH SCHOOL (ABOVE RIGHT)

◄ (left) Ilie Nastase's racket is returned to
him by a ball boy during a 1972 semi-final

◥ (above) Molly Bishop in action on the
Centre Court – ballgirls first appeared
alongside ball boys in 1986

ANDER-IN-CHIEF

HONORARY AND SERVICE STEWARDS

The distinctive appearance of the honorary and service stewards each year has become part of the tapestry of the Centre Court.

Honorary stewards are responsible for crowd management and act as 'hosts' to the public. Around 190 in number, the honorary stewards marshal the queues, inside and outside the grounds, advise and give help to visitors and supervise the seating of spectators. The presence of honorary stewards at Wimbledon originated in 1927, but it was not until 1950 that an Association of Wimbledon Honorary Stewards was formed.

They are assisted around the grounds by more than 500 volunteer service stewards on leave from the Army, Royal Navy, Royal Marines and Royal Air Force and also include a contingent provided by the London Fire Brigade. Many will have been on recent active duty abroad for their country. Service personnel were first used in 1946 and members of the London Fire Brigade in 1965.

A large majority of these voluntary stewards return each year. Around 250 stewards in total are allocated to the Centre Court. For all, the task is a matter of pride. They play a vital role.

◄ Hats off to the many servicemen and servicewomen whose voluntary role is essential to the success of The Championships

The Centre Court has, over the years, experienced a number of unplanned intrusions. Publicity seeking streakers or pranksters have, from time to time, been a particular and unwelcome nuisance. One of the more unusual was in 1957 during the men's doubles final. Helen Jarvis of Croydon invaded the Centre Court, shouting and (perhaps ahead of her time) waving a banner in her campaign for a new world banking system. The message on the banner began with the words "God Save Our Queen". The intruder was escorted from the court by the Referee and a policeman. The Queen watched the incident from the Royal Box.

REFEREE

The Referee is another familiar sight on and around the Centre Court – arriving with extraordinary timing at the back of Centre Court at the first sign of rain, settling on occasions a particularly troublesome player/umpire dispute and entering the Centre Court on finals day to greet the champion and the runner-up with a kind word.

The Referee's principal challenge, though, is the efficient and fair scheduling of matches to enable The Championships to be completed on time and in as orderly a manner as circumstances permit.

One important, and sometimes controversial, task is to schedule the programme for the Centre Court and other show-courts. The Referee consults the Club Chairman and the Order of Play Sub-Committee. The programme is usually announced around 6pm on the evening before play. Efficient and imaginative scheduling is crucial and complex. In deciding the daily order of play, a variety of interests must be balanced – including players, spectators, national and international TV, radio audiences and the print media. The interests of The Championships must come first.

Attractive top seeds with great crowd appeal naturally tend to get the lion's share of matches on the Centre Court (and No. 1 Court) especially when they have a good or close match in prospect. An effort is made,

◁ Championships' Referee, Andrew Jarrett, talks with the umpire about failing light during the fourth round match between Andy Murray and Richard Gasquet in 2008

in the interests of fairness, to make sure that the top seeds have reasonably similar numbers of appearances on the premier courts before they reach a crucial stage in The Championships. The interests of security and safety of the top players are also relevant. Although some preference may reasonably be given to British players where appropriate, this does not outweigh other factors more crucial to the interests and reputation of The Championships.

> "FOR ME, IT IS ONE OF THE GREAT CATHEDRALS OF WORLD SPORT. EVER SINCE MY FIRST VISIT THERE — FOR THE 1968 FINAL BETWEEN LAVER AND ROCHE — I'VE FELT A TINGLE DOWN MY SPINE WHENEVER I ENTER THE GREAT ARENA"
> ANDREW JARRETT. WIMBLEDON REFEREE, 2006–PRESENT

One tradition never changes. Since 1934, the opening match of The Championships has been played on the Centre Court by the men's singles champion from the previous year or, if he is not playing, by the runner-up. Likewise, the ladies' singles champion (or runner-up) from the previous year has normally opened play on the Centre Court on the first Tuesday.

Now, from 2009 onwards, the Referee has a new decision amongst his responsibilities – when to close (or open) the retractable roof.

MILITARY BAND

We end with the band. A military band has become a familiar and welcome sight before play on the final Saturday and Sunday.

The first military band to entertain the public was on the opening day of The Championships in 1926 but the modern practice of entertaining early arrivals to the Centre Court on the two finals days commenced in 1964.

Exceptionally, the band played for five days in 1977, Centenary Year. In 2000 the Band of the Scots Guards played on the first Saturday for the occasion of the Millennium Parade of Champions.

The band of the Honourable Artillery Company performing on Centre Court on the last day of the 2008 Championships ➤

LOUISE BROUGH d. MARGARET DU PONT

10	1	10		
8	6	8		

Of the great American women who dominated Wimbledon in the post war years, Louise Brough and Margaret du Pont were two of the most successful. Both were accomplished serve volleyers and both had already won the title — du Pont (née Osborne) in 1947 and Brough the following year. Friends and doubles partners, they were also great rivals. Who would prevail in their 1949 final?

MISS BROUGH'S SECOND VICTORY IN AN EPIC FINAL

Lawn Tennis and Badminton
15th July 1949
By John Dorey

The singles final was between the two "Queens" of modern women's tennis, Miss Brough and Mrs. du Pont. They battled for just under two hours for the ladies' crown in an epic final and Miss Brough retained her title because she was just a shade more consistent in the key games.

Mrs. du Pont staged a remarkable recovery in the first set after being 0-4 down and climbed to set point four times when leading 5-4 by resolute attack from the net. Somehow the champion staved her off and in a neck-and-neck struggle they reached eight-all before the holder cut down her errors to win two games for the set.

Mrs. du Pont was on top throughout the second set, punching some fine drives down the lines and volleying with power and precision.

It was not possible to identify the winner until the last ball had been struck in the 18 game third set. Rallies were few and far between in the high pressure net attack exploited by both ladies. Mrs. du Pont was in the lead up to 3-2 and again at 6-5. Sterling ground stroke play saved Miss Brough at 30-all in the next game and she was never again headed until the end came at 10-8.

8	16	3	8	12
6	18	6	6	10

Next, an unforgettable third round match from 1953. Budge Patty of the US (the 1950 French and Wimbledon champion) was playing the self-exiled Czech Jaroslav Drobny, now an Egyptian citizen. The battle raged for four and a quarter hours and ended in gathering darkness at 9.17 pm with both men exhausted.

DROBNY BEATS PATTY IN GREATEST EVER BATTLE

SURVIVES 6 MATCH POINTS IN 4¼ HOURS

The Daily Telegraph
26th June 1953
By Lance Tingay

Wimbledon should have ended tonight. Never in the history of the Championships has a match been waged more worthy of the greatest of all lawn tennis finals than the third round match in which Jaroslav Drobny, the former Czech, beat the 1950 champion, Budge Patty.

Only the 15,000 packed in the stadium can forever retell the breathless excitement of the champagne nature of lawn tennis; of the piquant fluctuations of the fortunes of two desperately heroic men; of the caprices of the goddess of luck; or of the stark drama of two players fighting the menace of encroaching cramp. The tall slender American was finally holding the upper part of his right leg between each rally, his face writhed in agony. Drobny, also almost ready to drop, only just outlasted his gallant rival.

This was the longest singles ever played in The Championships. It was a clash of artists with Drobny the worker in oils against the

more delicate water colourist. Never for a moment did the standard fall below the super fine and even when both were playing in a semi daze the quality of their instinctive strokes and their superb control of length and direction were maintained in the highest degree.

And so they came to the never-to-be-forgotten final set. Drobny built his lead into 3-1 and began sprinting up and down the baseline between the rallies to relieve oncoming cramp. Very soon after this Patty broke back and stood within a point of victory. They ran neck and neck to 10-all. The end was near.

The last few games were played in the dim light of dusk. Patty failed to hold his service. Drobny thus led 11-10 with his delivery to come. It was a love game to Drobny.

MAUREEN CONNOLLY d. DORIS HART

8	7			
6	5			

Maureen Connolly had already become the Wimbledon champion the previous year at the tender age of 17 and arrived in 1953 as the champion in Australia and France. A supreme baseliner and utterly ruthless as a match player, this time she was up against her great friend and 1951 champion, Doris Hart. It was a final of the highest quality. Connolly's victory would become the third leg of the first Grand Slam ever achieved by a woman.

MISS CONNOLLY WINS A GREAT FINAL

BETTER THAN SUZANNE LENGLEN?

The Sunday Times
5th July 1953
By Susan Noel

Miss Maureen Connolly (U.S.) today won the championship here for the second time beating Miss Doris Hart (U.S.) in a match which must rank as one of the greatest women's finals ever played at this meeting.

Both players were right on top of their form. Miss Hart had obviously planned to play the youthful champion from the back of the court, a campaign she stuck to throughout, and her ability to half-volley from the baseline stood her in good stead.

Up to 3-all in the first set the two players were driving to the line with amazing speed and exactitude. At this point Miss Connolly hit faster and faster and deeper and deeper. It looked as if she had acquired the Lenglen habit of making her opponents calculate their chances against her in terms of games and points rather than in sets and matches (on her way to the final Miss Connolly lost only eight games in the ten sets she played).

In the second set Miss Connolly stuck to her ruthlessness and got ahead with 3-1. Miss Hart made her final thrust, and at four-all, after a game of six deuces with each

player sharing equally the advantage points, Miss Connolly got the lead, held it, and at 6-5 won a love game for the match.

It is always amusing, if not profitable, to compare champions of one generation with those of another. One begins to feel that Miss Connolly has a real claim to be nominated the greatest of them all.

LEW HOAD d. KEN ROSEWALL

6	4	7	6
2	6	5	4

Australia's incredible tennis "twins", Lew Hoad and Ken Rosewall, were both from New South Wales. They had been junior rivals and had set new standards of achievement for tennis teenagers on the international stage in the 1950s. Now, aged 21, they met in the 1956 final.

The Times
7th July 1956
By Our Lawn Tennis Correspondent

L. A. Hoad became the new champion yesterday at Wimbledon, at the age of 21, when he beat K.R. Rosewall, another Australian of the same age, by 6-2, 4-6, 7-5, 6-4 in a glorious final, perhaps as good as any since the war.

As a spectacle in point of variety, speed and accuracy of stroke, and in swiftness of movement that was forever lending a thrill to the rallies, it is hard to think of a rival to this match. Moreover, to all this, the excitement as to who would win was instanced by the loser's first getting from 2-4 down to 5-4 in the third set and later leading 4-1 in the fourth.

Yet, for all this, there was that deep-down feeling that the winner would be Hoad. He had shown his full powers of attack in a devastating spell from two-all to win the first set. There was then a murmur of "What on earth can anyone do against that?" So it seems that he must always have that store of powerful energy to bring out when it is really needed, which he certainly did at the end. It was remarkable the amount of top spin which he imparted to his forehand and backhand drives, some of which sped past Rosewall at an alarming speed.

For a moment in the fourth set, there were visions of a five-setter. But not so, Hoad began to assume giant stature, and produced service aces almost at will and, if not, his other variety spun so viciously that even Rosewall could not compete. A spark came from the embers with Rosewall's gallant defence but Hoad put paid to this and set the seal on his triumph with a love game.

Hoad will go down as a memorable champion for his beauty of movement and hitting, and for this match alone.

HOAD BECOMES NEW WIMBLEDON CHAMPION
ROSEWALL BEATEN IN GLORIOUS FINISH

TECHNOLOGY & MEDIA

2.50
ROLEX
0.39
SETS GAMES POINTS
MISS S. WILLIAMS
4 40
MISS V. WILLIAMS
4 40
S. WILLIAMS
V. WILLIAMS

THE CENTRE COURT may seem traditional on the surface but as Billie Jean King has remarked: "*Nothing has changed at Wimbledon, and yet everything has.*" It is innovation behind the scenes that helps Wimbledon to remain the world's premier tennis tournament.

SCOREBOARDS/VIDEO SCREENS

The scoreboards are a vital and visual part of the 'design' of the Centre Court – including those on the outside of the building overlooking the main public concourses. Instantly, they keep the 15,000 watching spectators in touch with the score, as well as everyone around the ground and millions of viewers worldwide.

In 1922 there were just two manually operated scoreboards, one at each side of the court in line with the net. These showed the names of the players, the server and the score in sets and games. In 1924, a larger V-shaped, double scoreboard was introduced at the side, high above the standing area on the west side. Then in 1928 the scoreboards were positioned in the north-west and south-east corners of the court where they remain today.

Electric scoreboards were introduced in 1929, additionally showing the score in points. Spectators and players were so delighted with them that new enlarged scoreboards were commissioned and these also recorded full details of previous sets. Continuous improvements have been taking place ever since.

Scoreboards and the point-by-point screens around the grounds were, in 2006, linked for the first time directly to the umpire's handheld computer and updated automatically. The score is seen, in a matter of seconds, worldwide.

"SINCE UMPIRES WON'T ANNOUNCE THE SCORE UNTIL THE CROWD HAS STOPPED CLAPPING, SOMEONE IN PERU CAN SEE THE SCORE FROM CENTRE COURT BEFORE THE PEOPLE WHO ARE ACTUALLY THERE EVEN HEAR IT ANNOUNCED"
IBM, OFFICIAL INFORMATION TECHNOLOGY SUPPLIER

◄ The new scoreboards in operation during the 40th minute of the 2008 ladies' singles final

◥ The old scoreboard about to announce victory for Bjorn Borg over John McEnroe in 1980

HAWK-EYE

Technology has increasingly been introduced to the Centre Court scenery to help resolve difficult line-call decisions. The first umpire aid was 'Cyclops' (full name: CPE Service Line Monitor). This made its debut in 1980 – when Ilie Nastase tried to argue with it! Cyclops transmitted infra-red rays across the court in order to make close service line-calls but it is no longer used on the Centre Court following the introduction of 'Hawk-Eye'.

Named after its inventor Paul Hawkins, Hawk-Eye is an electronic review system which was used officially for the first time in 2007 on Centre Court (and No. 1 Court) to allow line-calls to be reviewed by the umpire during a match following a challenge by one of the players. In order for the players, officials and spectators to see the replays, large video screens were installed. Since 2008 enlarged screens, or video boards, enable the scores and Hawk-Eye replays – and other video information – to be displayed in one location.

⋏ A linesman holds the box that activates 'Cyclops'

Hawk-Eye operates through ten high speed cameras around the perimeter roof of the Centre Court which track the ball as it flies through the air. A computer captures the image from each camera, combines all this information and reconstructs the most likely trajectory, statistically, of the ball. This information is then sent to the control room (high up at the northern end of the Centre Court) where the graphic images are produced which are seen on the screens and on television. A supervisor from the International Tennis Federation sits with the technicians, to ensure that the correct shot is being analysed.

Under present rules, players have unlimited opportunity to challenge line-calls but once three incorrect challenges have been made by a player in a set, he or she cannot challenge again until the next set. If the set goes to a tiebreak or advantage set, players are given additional opportunities to challenge.

⋏ Spectators enjoy being able to see the Hawk-Eye decisions displayed on the two courtside scoreboards

SPEED OF SERVE

A radar gun measuring the 'speed of service' was first used on the Centre Court for television in 1991. It was not until 1999, however, that display units were installed at ground level at both ends of the court so that spectators were able to see immediately the speed of a player's service.

A specially designed radar sensor, positioned at the back of the court behind the server at each end, measures the speed over the first few feet after the server's striking of the ball. The data is transmitted to the IBM control room and the result shown on the visual display unit courtside.

The fastest men's serve so far recorded on the Centre Court is 145 mph by Andy Roddick in 2004 and again in 2005. The fastest recorded woman's serve is 129 mph by Venus Williams in 2008.

⋏ Rafael Nadal has just returned a 113 mph serve during the 2008 Championships

OFFICIAL SUPPLIERS

The Centre Court is one of the very few major world sporting events which is free of overt commercialisation in the stadium (such as perimeter or courtside advertising). The Club believes that this policy enhances the image and character of The Championships.

Instead, the Club has developed a range of mutually beneficial 'official supplier' agreements with a range of well-known brands. Many of these are long term relationships. Official suppliers provide goods and services necessary for the staging of The Championships or which meet the Club's objective of improving the quality of the service provided to the players, spectators and the media.

Many of these official suppliers are 'at work' in Centre Court as well as throughout the grounds: Rolex appears on the scoreboard and clocks as Official Timekeeper; IBM is the Official Information Technology Supplier; Robinsons is the Official Still Soft Drink (an association going back to 1934 with a long tradition of the Robinsons Barley Water bottle on the umpire's chair on court);

⋏ Robinsons Barley Water, always present on the umpire's chair

Evian is the Official Bottled Water; Polo Ralph Lauren is the Official Outfitter; and Slazenger provide the Official Ball and other court equipment (as they have done since 1902).

Others associated with operations include: HSBC (Official Banking Partner and sponsor of the ticket resale operation) and Hertz (Official Car Supplier providing transport for the players).

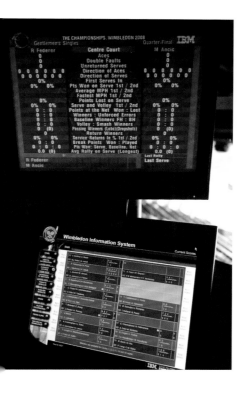

TELEVISION

The Championships at Wimbledon are the world's most widely seen tennis tournament. In 2009 around 12,000 hours of coverage were broadcast to more than 180 countries — reaching a global cumulative audience of some 375 million – and there is a special magic to the Centre Court not only for spectators but also for the millions watching at home.

During the fortnight, in and around the Centre Court a whole team of television staff is working to convey the pictures seen by millions of viewers worldwide. The commentators can be glimpsed around the court in their commentary boxes in the top tier of the Centre Court or, more prominently in the case of the BBC and NBC (the current network US broadcaster), at lower level in the two boxes in the south-east and north-west corners of the Centre Court. Many are well-known and popular ex-players.

Supporting this coverage, there are around 16 strategically placed TV camera positions within the Centre Court, all feeding into the state of the art Broadcast Centre neighbouring the Centre Court on the other side of St. Mary's Walk.

BBC radio coverage of Centre Court began in 1927 and television followed in 1937. The first scheduled colour television transmission in Britain, on BBC2, took place at Wimbledon during the 1967 Championships. The eight-man professional tournament held in August that year was also broadcast daily on BBC2 as part of the BBC's programme to launch colour television in the UK.

The BBC is presently the host broadcaster, as well as the UK rights holder, acting for more than 40 other international networks. The 2008 men's final attracted a peak audience in the UK of 13.3 million viewers. The largest audience worldwide was almost certainly for the 2008 semi-final between Serena Williams and China's Zheng Jie. An estimated 100 million people in China watched.

On the two finals days, TV itself becomes one of the direct participants on the stage. Since 2000, the BBC's Sue Barker has interviewed the finalists after their matches.

◁ BBC Television has broadcast from the Centre Court every year from 1937

◮ Tim Henman swaps racket for microphone in 2008 for the BBC

◮ A remotely controlled camera on Centre Court, one of nine cameras used by the BBC for the principal matches

PRESS, RADIO AND PHOTOGRAPHERS

Wimbledon is the focus of the worldwide sporting media during The Championships. Around 900 journalists, radio reporters and photographers are granted accreditation. They represent daily, evening and Sunday newspapers, international wire services and news agencies and include licensed radio reporters and specialist writers for tennis/sport magazines. The press box is in the north-west stand of the Centre Court and even experienced journalists are still moved by working in this historic location.

More than 250 photographers are accredited and entry to the Centre Court is closely controlled. In total, there are now over 80 camera positions in the Centre Court most of which are in the pits on the east and west sides of the court.

Technology lies at the heart of the service. For 2004, the Club introduced a Wi-Fi system (Wireless Fidelity: a local area wireless internet network) in the Centre Court (and No. 1 Court) which enables press and photographers to transmit data easily within the grounds and across the world wide web. Using a digital camera, a photographer can shoot pictures of a dramatic moment on Centre Court and immediately transmit them to his or her picture editor's desk. A photograph of Tim Henman diving for a shot in 2004 (below) made it to the front page of *The Times* within 59 seconds of his

◄ Press photographers take their customary final photographs

◄ One of the two photographers' pits on either side of Centre Court

> "WHEN I FIRST WALKED INTO THE CENTRE COURT IT WAS MUCH BIGGER THAN I HAD VISUALISED... AND QUIETER. JUST BEFORE THE START OF A BIG MATCH, WHEN IT IS PACKED WITH SPECTATORS, IT'S RATHER LIKE A CHURCH... A REVERENTIAL PLACE RADIATING PEACE AND TRANQUILLITY. EVEN NOW, COMING BACK EACH YEAR, IT STILL TAKES MY BREATH AWAY"
>
> NEIL HARMAN, THE TIMES

landing on the court. Technology has made life easier for all concerned.

The session on each finals day at the back of the Centre Court, with the mass of photographers jostling for position after the end of the trophy presentation, has become a familiar sight – followed by the champion's lap of honour for the benefit of the many amateur photographers in the crowd.

◄ (middle) This picture of Tim Henman was on the front page of The Times within a minute of being taken

◄ Photos are beamed from Centre Court into the media centre and from there across the globe

ANGELA MORTIMER d. CHRISTINE TRUMAN

4	6	7
6	4	5

DRAMATIC END TO BRITAIN'S MEMORABLE WIMBLEDON

At last, in 1961, all the long years of waiting for another British champion were ended; yes, two British players in the final! This was the first all-British women's final at Wimbledon since 1914. Angela Mortimer was seeking her life's ambition at the age of 29 against the popular favourite, Christine Truman. It was an emotional match.

The Times

10th July 1961

By Our Lawn Tennis Correspondent

Wimbledon 1961 was a fiesta of surprise and entertainment. For the first time in nearly half a century there came the 1914 echo of an all-British women's final.

The past suggested a battle of the tactical brain of the frail Miss Mortimer against the power of Miss Truman. In the event Miss Truman played one of the most thoughtful — and gallant — matches of her career, only to have the last prize snatched away by the fates.

Already a set up and then leading 4-3, with advantage against Miss Mortimer's service, Miss Truman suddenly had to check and change direction to recover a net cord stroke by her subtle opponent. That was the cruel moment of decision; she suffered cramp and the next five games melted away in a flash.

If Miss Truman naturally won universal pity there should be sympathy, too, for Miss Mortimer. It is never easy to win in such a situation. Seeded seventh, she is to be congratulated for coming unobtrusively and efficiently through the field over a hard fortnight. She knew her own strengths and weaknesses and those of her opponents and she made her plans accordingly. Hers was a

triumph of mind over matter.

Miss Truman, if never again at the peak, recovered sufficiently to make a stupendous challenge at the end as the Centre Court rocked in its excitement. She recovered to 4-all in the final set and now, on court and up to the highest rims of the Centre Court, the tension became

almost unbearable. Here was one of the most dramatic women's finals for a long time. Back and forth the struggle had swayed and now at last the end was reached.

Miss Mortimer, detached, persistent, always driving or lobbing to a perfect length, varying her game, was the new champion.

MARIA BUENO d. MARGARET SMITH

6	7	6
4	9	3

The 1964 ladies' final saw the reigning champion, Margaret Smith, against the elegant queen of Brazilian tennis, Maria Bueno. Their rivalry enthralled followers of the women's game for years. This was a tremendous battle of power against finesse.

Stylish Miss Bueno regains her crown

**The Sunday Times
5th July 1964
By Henry Raven**

'The perfect final' was the perfect final. In 90 minutes of the most wonderful lawn tennis seen at Wimbledon for years Maria Bueno regained her title by beating the holder, Margaret Smith.

It was a breathtaking performance. Miss Bueno can never have played better. There were moments when she made mistakes but she seldom played a shot in the whole long tense match that was not graceful, elegant and purposeful.

The Brazilian's art blunted Miss Smith's power. Swift, searing and graceful strokes captured vital points from her, and all her speed and strength, her great physical fitness, could not prevent Miss Bueno gaining a victory which moved the Centre Court to a peak of emotion and excitement.

Miss Bueno won the first set after losing two breaks of service, and in the second she failed with two more for a break at 5-5. Brilliant inconsistencies are as much part of her game as superb volleys and smashes, but she won this afternoon because she sustained the beautiful power of her play for so long.

Miss Bueno's challenge in the early games was superb. She started as though the first green grass of the Centre Court belonged to her. The great question in the later part of the match was whether she had the strength and stamina to maintain the quality of this attack against the formidable Australian.

The end was almost the only part of the match that was not artistic. Miss Bueno's last shot was a half-volley

which looked as if it was off the wood. It dropped like a stone. The Centre Court rose to Miss Bueno, and she wept. This afternoon she was supreme again on the court where she always plays her best.

"IF YOU CAN MEET WITH TRIUMPH AND DISASTER
AND TREAT THOSE TWO IMPOSTORS JUST THE SAME"

OFF STAGE

E NOW GO 'behind the scenes' and explore the Centre Court building away from the court itself. We start by following in the steps of the players themselves. It is a journey that every aspiring young tennis player, boy or girl, dreams of taking one day.

◁ A service steward standing outside the entrance to the men's dressing room

Roger Federer sits opposite his locker on the eve of the 2008 Championships ➢

◄ The elegantly furnished lady members' dressing room used by the top ranking players during The Championships

One of the six bathrooms in the ladies' dressing room ➤

Another view of the inside of the ladies' dressing room ➤

DRESSING ROOMS

The dressing rooms are on the west side of the Centre Court building. There are three men's and three ladies' dressing rooms. Lockers of Club members are emptied two weeks before The Championships. The top-ranked players, including former champions, are allocated to the relevant members' dressing room on the first floor. Each player is given his or her own locker.

The principal ladies' dressing room has pride of place in terms of its decoration and style. The men's room, while comfortable, is more simply furnished.

A long established custom, on men's final day, has been for the head attendant in the men's dressing room to carry the bags of the two men's singles finalists on to the Centre Court; a proud moment for him and a tradition much enjoyed by watching members of the Club.

A Club official is responsible for ensuring that the players are ready and waiting to go onto the Centre Court. He or she also ensures that the players are wearing correct clothing within the rules, both as regards colour and advertising.

Then, escorted by the official, the players make their way along a corridor, with photographs of former champions lining the walls. Near the entrance to the Royal Box, they then descend the staircase into the entrance hall.

⋏ Traditionally the senior dressing room attendant leads the men's singles finalists on court and carries their equipment bags. In 2007 that honour fell to Douglas Dickson

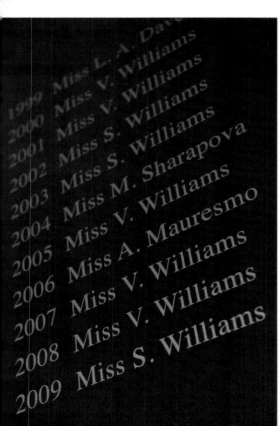

ENTRANCE HALL

The Club's entrance hall was completely refurbished in 2002. It now incorporates twin dog- leg staircases. At the top is a landing with access to the Royal Box. At the bottom lies the entrance to the Centre Court.

Over the entrance to the court, through which the players pass, is the inscription from Rudyard Kipling's poem *If*.

> "IF YOU CAN MEET WITH TRIUMPH AND DISASTER AND TREAT THOSE TWO IMPOSTORS JUST THE SAME..."

The original board bearing the inscription was presented to the Club by Lord Curzon in the autumn of 1923. It was replaced just prior to the 1995 Championships and again when the Clubhouse was refurbished in 2002. The original board is on display in the Wimbledon Lawn Tennis Museum.

The players pass the two roll of honours' boards of past singles champions, before proceeding through etched glass doors. They wait briefly in the players' waiting room before entering the Centre Court immediately below the Royal Box.

▲ The lists of men's and ladies' champions on the walls of the entrance hall just outside the main entrance to the Centre Court

◄ Every year, on finals day, the name of the winner is added to the list before the new champion has left the court

THE WALK TO THE COURT

The Club official responsible for ensuring that players arrive as smoothly as possible on Centre Court is sometimes known as 'the Master of Ceremonies'. Dan Bloxham now performs that role for the men, Jane Poynder for the ladies.

Dan explains: "*On a typical day, between 11.30am and 12 noon I begin checking that the players are in the correct dressing room or on the practice courts and let them know the timeline for the first match on Centre Court. This is due to start exactly at 1pm, so at 12.30pm I make my second visit to the players' dressing room. I make sure that both players are there and ready to leave for 12.55 pm, wearing appropriate clothing and correct sized sponsorship patches. At 12.57 pm we leave the locker room and start the two and a half minute walk along the corridor, down the stairs, under the Kipling quote to wait at the door to Centre Court with 30 seconds to spare before the clock ticks to 1 pm and I lead the players out for the first match of the day.*"

For subsequent matches, Dan makes contact with the players as soon as the previous match goes on to Centre Court. The players are asked to be ready to leave the dressing rooms the moment that match finishes and they are reminded to check the ball-by-ball screens to help their timing. "*During the first week all the dressing rooms are full with players, coaches and physios so it can be a challenge to find your player!*" remarks Dan.

The procedure on finals day is different. Dan himself feels the extra tension and excitement. There are only two players and their coaches left in the main dressing room. The players leave the dressing room at 1.50pm and the finalists each do a short interview with the BBC just outside the dressing room in front of the walkway window. Then the drama begins.

"*The walk to the Centre Court on finals day has a certain magic about it,*" says Dan. "*The BBC cameraman walks a metre in front of me, the players just behind. As we walk, All England Club members move to the sides to allow the players through amidst an air of quiet yet intense excitement. With two minutes to go we arrive at the bottom of the Clubhouse stairs and are greeted by the Chairman and Chief Executive of the Club and the tournament Referee, who wish the finalists good luck. We wait by the door to Centre Court for the clock to tell 2 pm., the doors open and we are surrounded by cameras, noise from the crowd and an electric anticipation as I lead the players the 15 steps to the edge of the grass. As the finalists pass, I too wish them luck.*"

Serena Williams leads her sister, Venus, towards the main entrance to Centre Court prior to their 2008 final ➤

CHAMPIONSHIP TROPHIES

If they glance to their right side on their way down the stairs from the dressing rooms to the door to Centre Court, the players see, in the entrance hall and set alongside the staircases, two tall glass trophy cabinets containing the trophies for all the main events.

The Challenge Cup is the famous Wimbledon men's singles trophy. It was purchased by the Club in 1887 at a cost of 100 guineas. It is a perpetual trophy which can 'never become the property of the winner' (unlike its predecessor which was won outright by William Renshaw). The Cup, which is made of silver gilt, stands 18½ inches high and has a diameter of 7½ inches. Around the bowl are engraved the dates and names of the champions. The inscription on the Cup reads:

> "The All England
> Lawn Tennis Club
> Single Handed
> Championship
> of the World"

The ladies' singles trophy, dating from 1886, is a magnificent partly gilded silver salver, known as the 'Rosewater Dish' or the 'Venus Rosewater Dish'. The salver is 18¼ inches in diameter. The trophy bears no inscription other than engraving showing the dates and names of all the champions. Dates and names from 1884 to 1957 are to be found around the

⋏ The Venus Rosewater dish, a perpetual challenge trophy, carries the name of every lady champion

"THE MOMENT WHEN I COULD LIFT THE TROPHY INTO THE AIR FOR THE FIRST TIME WAS JUST MAGIC. IT WAS UNREAL. IT'S SO BEAUTIFUL, MADE FROM GOLD, NOT TOO HEAVY, NOT TOO LIGHT, JUST RIGHT..."
ROGER FEDERER

inside of the bowl and from 1958 to date around the outside of the bowl.

On each finals day, the singles trophies are engraved with the winner's name immediately at the end of the match. Roman Zoltowski comes from Poland every year to engrave the trophies. He and his assistant work by eye, in a room near the entrance to the Centre Court, using traditional hand engraving tools.

The honours board is actually updated by the time the presentation ceremony has ended and the players re-emerge into the entrance hall.

The presentation ceremony on the Centre Court after the two singles finals has become a firm Wimbledon tradition. The practice originated in 1949 when the Duchess of Kent (as President of the Club) gave the men's singles trophy on court to Ted Schroeder. The following day, the ladies' doubles trophy was presented to Louise Brough and Margaret du Pont. From 1946 to 1948 the trophies were presented in the Royal Box. Previously, the trophies had not been presented in public, but occasionally the champions and runners-up were summoned to the Royal Box to receive the Royal congratulations.

Traditionally, the Royal presenter of the singles' trophies is escorted onto the court by the Chairman of the Club and the President of the LTA.

Prize money was introduced in 1968 following The Championships becoming an 'open' tournament for former professionals and amateurs alike. In 1968 the prize money was £2,000 for the winner of the men's singles and £750 for the winner of the ladies' singles. Since 2007, there has been equal prize money for men and women in all events. In 2009 the winner of each of the men's and ladies' singles received £850,000.

Master engraver Roman Zoltowski at work on finals day ➤

HAWKS & SPANIELS

One of the more unusual workers during The Championships is a Harris hawk trained by Wayne Davis, a full time falconer from Avian Control. A hawk (sometimes assisted by a falcon) visits the Club several times during the year to ward off local pigeons by warning them of a predator on the grounds, encouraging them to roost elsewhere. The practice started in 2000. Before that, the Centre Court was a favourite venue of the pigeons and play had previously been disturbed on a number of occasions.

The latest hawk entrusted with this task is Rufous. Rufous or his colleague flies for one hour, from around 9am every morning of The Championships before the gates open.

Other early workers on Centre Court include a team of Metropolitan Police 'sniffer' dogs who check the area every morning as part of the security operation before the public enter the grounds.

⋏ (top) Rufous the hawk spreads his wings while (above) Charlie, a Springer Spaniel sniffer dog, inspects between the Centre Court seats

⋖ (far left) Rufous inspecting one of the new roof trusses

MEMBERS' AREAS

Off the corridor from the dressing rooms to the front of the Clubhouse lie rooms for use by the members of the Club and also, during The Championships, councillors of the Lawn Tennis Association. They provide an opportunity for a cup of tea, or perhaps something stronger, and a chance to catch up with results around the ground. Some members simply enjoy the view from the balcony over the southern part of the grounds towards St. Mary's Church.

ROYAL BOX LANDING AND DINING ROOM

At the top of the steps leading from, and overlooking, the entrance hall is a balconied landing area – used as a lounge and bar for Club members during the rest of the year. During The Championships, it becomes the Royal Box landing where guests for the day are greeted. Tea is served on the balcony overlooking the southern end of the ground.

Further to the east is the Club members' dining room where, during The Championships, lunch is served for Royal Box guests prior to the start of play.

COMMITTEE

Off the entrance hall on the ground floor, to either side, are the offices of the Club Chairman, the Chief Executive and the Club Secretary and assistant staff. Nearby, a plaque honours members of the Club who died in the two World Wars. On either side of the entrance to the court there are two meeting rooms.

◄ The beautifully inlaid conference table in the Club's boardroom

The Committee of Management, led by the Club Chairman, has overall responsibility for the running of The Championships. It comprises 12 elected members of the All England Lawn Tennis & Croquet Club and seven representatives appointed by the Lawn Tennis Association.

Day-to-day management is carried out by an executive team led by the Club's Chief Executive reporting to the Committee of Management and, where appropriate, various sub-committees covering different major aspects of the operations of The Championships (such as finance, ground, press and broadcasting, marketing, order of play, ticketing, information technology, transport, catering and security and risk issues).

The Club employs a permanent staff of around 140 engaged on Club and Championship affairs. During The Championships, approximately 4,500 temporary staff are engaged either by the Club or by the various independent contractors (such as security, transport and catering) engaged on delivering the services necessary to stage The Championships.

Running The Championships is a responsibility to sport. The major part of the financial surplus from the staging of The Championships is, under arrangements agreed between the Club and the Lawn Tennis Association (LTA), allocated to the LTA for the development of the sport at all levels in Great Britain.

CATERING AND SHOP

As the Centre Court building spreads outwards, it incorporates catering and shop facilities designed to meet the demands of the modern-day audience at a premier sporting event. All have been completely built or substantially refurbished during the recent modernisation of the Centre Court structure as a whole.

The public Tea Lawn on the ground floor to the east is quaintly named after the original days when spectators did take tea on a lawn. Re-built and extended, it provides modern catering space for the public. Nearby, and not far from a newly-built Wimbledon shop, is now the public Wingfield Restaurant which seats 450 guests in some style. On the floors above, on the east and north sides of the building, are high quality restaurant, bar and lounge areas for debenture holders

◀ Hulling the strawberries – all 28,000 kilos of them – is a considerable task

⋏ During The Championships the corks are popped on some 17,000 bottles of champagne

⋏ (right) A table awaits in the debenture holders' restaurant

– many with attractive views and balconies.

All are served by kitchens within the Centre Court building and organised by outside caterers appointed by the Club – for many years, Facilities Management Catering (FMC) – whose office lies within the south-east depths of the Centre Court building.

From the earliest days at Worple Road, Wimbledon has been associated with 'strawberry teas'. Today, approximately 28,000 kilos of strawberries are consumed by visitors during The Championships. Strawberry "hulling" takes place in a back-room under the Centre Court.

RADIO WIMBLEDON

Tucked in on the north-west side of the Centre Court complex is the Club's own radio station for The Championships, Radio Wimbledon — available on the 87.7 FM frequency and reaching an area of up to four miles around the grounds. A separate channel (96.3 FM) broadcasts commentary from the Centre Court especially for the benefit of those with a visual or hearing impairment.

THE OTHER 50 WEEKS...

The Centre Court's life is centred on The Championships. Whilst the grounds at Wimbledon are the active home for members of the All England Lawn Tennis & Croquet Club during the remainder of the year, there is traditionally no other play on the Centre Court (or No. 1 Court).

There are two exceptions. Four lady members of the Club "play the court in" on the Saturday prior to The Championships. This also gives the ballboys and girls practice on the Centre Court and allows testing of the scoreboards, the speed of serve display and the public address system. On the Wednesday after the tournament, the Club Chairman invites members of the Club Committee and senior executives to an afternoon's tennis before the court is taken out of use.

A further exception in the past has been the use of the Centre Court for the final rounds of the Davis Cup when the Challenge Round was hosted by Great Britain in consecutive years from 1934 to 1937 (won by Great Britain on three occasions). The Centre Court was also used for the Wightman Cup matches between ladies' teams representing Great Britain and the USA in alternate years from 1924 to 1938. Any Davis Cup matches at Wimbledon have, more recently, been played on No. 1 Court.

The next major event for which the Centre Court will be used (along with other grass courts at the Club) outside The Championships will be the London Olympic Games in 2012. The courts will be handed over to the Olympic authorities for the tennis event immediately after the 2012 Championships. The grass courts will, of course, remain in the careful care of the Club's groundsman and staff.

The Centre Court building as a whole has an active life outside The Championships (when construction is not taking place). Dressing rooms, offices,

⚹ (top) An unusual winter scene – snow on the Centre Court

⚹ The court is "played in" by four lady members before the 2008 Championships

committee rooms, members' dining and bar areas are all in use.

During the remainder of the year outside The Championships, many a Club member will still go into the playing arena of the Centre Court and view it with affection and pride. It is an experience which may be shared by visitors to the Wimbledon Lawn Tennis Museum who now have access to a new viewing platform, known as *CentreCourt 360* (see page 181), directly within the Centre Court itself. Although empty and quiet, the Centre Court still resonates with memories of past matches and champions.

MEMORABLE MATCHES

PANCHO GONZALES d. CHARLIE PASARELL

22	1	16	6	11
24	6	14	3	9

BOOED GONZALES CHEERED AFTER MARATHON VICTORY

The opening day in 1969, the second year of open tennis, brought together the ageing lion, Pancho Gonzales, still fiercely competitive at 41, and American Davis Cup player Charlie Pasarell. Gonzales, the world's best player for most of the 1950s, had spent 15 long years in the twilight world of professional tennis. Pasarell, aged 25, was at his peak. It became an unforgettable match.

The Daily Telegraph
26th June 1969
By Lance Tingay

Ricardo Gonzales, 41, who has never won the singles at Wimbledon and almost certainly never will, yesterday put himself into the annals of the championships as predominantly as a champion ever did.

On Tuesday night, when it was almost dark, Gonzales was booed as he left the Centre Court. Yesterday afternoon, when the same player had won one of the most memorable matches of all time, they cheered him as few players have been cheered before.

They could hardly have done less. The mighty Gonzales, always a giant in his standard of performance, came through a Wimbledon match that broke records of every sort.

He completed his unfinished business of the night before, when he was left trailing against his fellow American, Charlie Pasarell, 22-24 1-6. The road back was a long one and Gonzales, a hero in every step, made it.

He won the third, fourth and fifth sets on an unforgettable afternoon. He won a match in which he never led until the last two games, in which he was several times within a shot of losing (twice he recovered from 0-40 on his own delivery) and which on its completion gave

Wimbledon the longest singles both in number of games and duration. It lasted five hours 12 minutes in all, two hours and 20 minutes of that being taken up with what took place on Tuesday. And it was a contest of pristine quality.

This, despite its heroic standards, was only a first round match. It is one of the tragedies of lawn tennis that Wimbledon never saw Gonzales at his peak. But even at 41, Gonzales makes

other players look puny. This restless, fidgety giant dominates the court, his opponent and the whole scene.

Pasarell had played his heart out and he had played well. But the giant against him would not lie down. Someone had to yield to bring this unforgettable struggle to fruition and it was the younger man. Gonzales had refused to lose.

MEMORABLE MATCHES
ROD LAVER d. ARTHUR ASHE

2	6	9	6
6	2	7	0

It was the 1969 semi-final. The holder, Rod Laver, with that year's Australian and French titles already in his possession, was up against America's Arthur Ashe, winner of the previous year's US Open. Would Ashe's blistering form overcome the mighty Laver — or would the great Australian continue in his campaign for a second Grand Slam?

The Guardian

4th July 1969

By David Gray

Laver's thunder quells Ashe's lightning

Wimbledon came to its great confrontation yesterday.

Arthur Ashe, the US Open champion and the leader of the new generation, came up against Rod Laver, the holder, and the most professional of the professionals. For one set Ashe ravaged the court, breaking Laver's service three times with the fastest and fiercest returns of the week.

Then, gradually, Laver broke the force of the storm. Doggedly he asserted his strength. Forcefully he showed that his brilliancies were the more devastating.

In the end, after the most spectacular hour and a half of the week, Laver won 2-6 6-2 9-7 6-0. He took the last nine games and the fourth set lasted only 14 minutes. Ashe, the poised begetter of lawn tennis lightning, was destroyed, but his destruction was a work of art. The speed of the exchanges was breathtaking, the risks were fantastic, and the margins for error were infinitesimal.

The first set struck everyone dumb. Has Laver's service ever been captured three times running in a set? Afterwards Ashe said that he had never played as well in his life as he did in those eight games. His topspin backhands, in particular, were scarcely visible to the eye and hardly touchable by the racket.

Certainly, all the Centre Court's old inhabitants tried to remember a similar performance. In the end white haired gentlemen began to mutter about Vines achieving a similar pace and accuracy. Laver looked bleak and world weary, but with a champion's logic, and a champion's knowledge of his rivals, reckoned that Ashe could not continue to play with such flair and fury.

Laver began to find his range, and his service began to work up to full power. The force of Ashe's challenge stirred him to an equal ferocity. Three aces in the fifth game of the second set signalled his counter attack and in the next he broke for 4-2, and moved on for the set. From then on Laver was more in command than the American. Intermittently, there were gleams of dark, swift skill from Ashe, but for the most part Laver held the initiative.

At the end Laver's domination of the court — both mental and physical — was complete.

She had been knocking on the door for 13 years but always there had been someone in her way. In 1969 Britain's Ann Jones, now 30, knew there were not too many years of opportunity left. Her splendid semi-final win over the top seed Margaret Court gave her legion of supporters hope that this would be her year. In the final she would face the No. 2 seed Billie Jean King, the American who had beaten her in the final two years earlier.

Victory at last for Ann Jones

The Guardian
5th July 1969
By David Gray

When the British women win at Wimbledon, it is only after years of patience and disappointment. At 16 minutes past three yesterday afternoon Ann Jones, who had competed in the tournament for 13 years without winning any kind of title, watched Billie Jean King, the holder for the past three years, surrender the singles championship to her by 3-6 6-3 6-2 with a double fault.

The Centre Court erupted; Mrs. King, a member of the same professional troupe, climbed over the net to embrace her. Capt. Michael Gibson, the referee, kissed her and Princess Anne, taking the place of the Queen, who is ill, gave her the trophy. The journey to this success has been long and arduous, and if the victory at the end had not been spectacular, like her win over Margaret Court on Wednesday, the occasion had been full of emotion.

She herself regarded beating Mrs. Court as her principal achievement. That had been a good match, artistically right. The final had been a test of nerves, too much of an occasion for

either player to produce her best.

It looked at first as though Mrs. King, the supreme opportunist, would bustle her out of the match in her familiar fashion. In the first set Mrs. Jones was not getting in to volley as quickly as she had done against Mrs. Court and instead of hitting firmly she was tentative. She limped a little, too, because of a strained thigh muscle, a legacy of her semi-final. Everybody

seemed to be fearing the worst.

Suddenly Mrs. Jones recaptured the mood of her victory against Mrs. Court. When she had been in danger then she had attacked, and now, as she followed this policy again, the match swung towards her. For the British, the match was alight at last.

When it was over yesterday Mrs. King called her "the most underrated British player there has ever been".

MARGARET COURT d. BILLIE JEAN KING

14	11
12	9

The 1970 ladies' final between Billie Jean King and Margaret Court, two of the game's greatest champions, became a desperate battle of wills, every point being contested as if their lives depended on it! Although both were carrying injuries, they produced one of the most compelling contests ever seen on the Centre Court.

Mrs Court: only one more peak to climb

The Times
4th July 1970
By Rex Bellamy

Margaret Court, 27, became Wimbledon champion for the third time by beating Billie Jean King 14-12 11-9 in 2 hours, 27 minutes in a final that will be remembered as one of the greatest women's matches played anywhere. It had a thrilling beauty that chilled the blood and, in retrospect, still chills the blood.

It was the longest women's singles final in the history of The Championships; and the first set was the longest played by either sex in a Wimbledon singles final.

The only thing this match lacked was a sharp contrast in style and character. It had everything else in abundance. It was so good that it challenged belief. It still does.

Here were two gloriously gifted players at their best, or so close to it that the margin was irrelevant. They gave us a marvellous blend of athleticism and skill, courage and concentration, experience and wit. They moved each other about with remorseless haste. They hit a flashing stream of lovely shots. The match was punctuated throughout by rallies of wondrously varied patterns.

Every stroke, every tactical shift, was deeply tailored to the need of the moment. This was thoroughly professional tennis, the best the women's game could hope to produce. At the heart of the struggle lay each player's superb qualities as a competitor. They never gave an inch. When an inch was taken from them, they had the resilience to win it back.

Mrs. Court's service and smash, and her backhand drives, volleys and lobs, were almost flawless. On the forehand, both drive and volley, she was more tentative and vulnerable. Mrs. King's crosscourt backhand made a rasping contribution to the day's winners. Like Mrs Court, she was mercilessly sound overhead.

This was majestic and powerful tennis, the right stuff for a King and a Court to play before a crowd including three princesses and the Prime Minister.

In the second set, as in the first, Mrs. King held her service five times to stay in the battle. At the sixth time of asking, she had five more match points against her. Four she boldly saved. Then Mrs. Court came up on a backhand, Mrs. King's response found the net, and it was over.

GREAT CHAMPIONS

THE PAST 40 YEARS

CHRIS EVERT | 1974, 1976, 1981

CHRIS EVERT had been prepared from an early age for stardom by her father Jimmy, a teaching professional in Fort Lauderdale, Florida, and her first Wimbledon success came aged 19.

For nearly two decades, her consummate steadiness and shrewd courtcraft, together with a double-fisted backhand that set the fashion for a new generation, brought massive success. She prospered at all the Grand Slams winning the French singles title seven times (a record), the US title six times, the Wimbledon singles three times and the Australian twice. In 56 Grand Slam singles events she failed on only four occasions to reach at least the semi-final stage, a prodigious record.

Chris's three singles titles at Wimbledon occurred in 1974, 1976 and 1981 when she defeated Olga Morozova, Evonne Cawley and Hana Mandlikova respectively in the final. Apart from these occasions, Chris contested seven other singles finals, losing to Billie Jean King and Evonne Cawley

◄ Chris Evert at the start of a brilliant career which would bring her three singles titles from ten finals

◄ The Duke of Kent leads the applause for Chris Evert's success in 1974

once each and to Martina Navratilova as many as five times, all in the 1980s, when Navratilova was at her peak.

Ball control and command of length were the classic ingredients of Chris's mastery. If best on the slow rubble of what used to be called hard courts in Britain and clay in Europe and the USA, she was equally a champion on any surface. Her consistency was measured by a winning sequence of 125 matches on clay. In all, she captured 154 singles titles, 18 of them Grand Slams. From 1972 to 1989 she never appeared in the world ranking lists lower than no. 4 and for a total of 262 weeks held the no. 1 position, ending the year atop the rankings on five occasions.

This much-loved champion revived the prestige of the traditional values of the women's game based on sound groundstrokes and at the same time defied orthodoxy with her double-fisted backhand. This she turned into common practice all round the world. A model of consistency and outstanding for her sportsmanship, she stands as an exemplary champion.

"THE GREATEST FEELING IN THE WORLD IS HOLDING THAT PLATE ABOVE YOUR HEAD"
CHRIS EVERT

BJÖRN BORG | 1976, 1977, 1978, 1979, 1980

NEVER IN THE history of lawn tennis did any player accomplish so much and in so brief a time as the Swede, Björn Borg. He was more coolly dominating and ruthless at Wimbledon than any previous modern challenger, precociously successful on clay courts in Paris, clinically efficient in the Davis Cup and entirely a sporting phenomenon. Only the US title was to escape his grasp: he lost in the final four times.

Having won the junior tournament at Wimbledon in 1972 aged 16, it was in 1976 at his fourth attempt that Borg wove the first major strands in his unique Wimbledon tapestry. He lost a set to no-one, his victims including Guillermo Vilas, the hard-serving Roscoe Tanner in the semis and the touch genius Ilie Nastase in the final. It would not be until 1981 that he next lost at Wimbledon. The span was from 1st July 1975, when Ashe beat him in the quarter-finals, to 4th July 1981 with McEnroe his victor in the final: 41 matches in a continuity of victory and five successive titles!

After the first, Borg's subsequent titles were more onerously gained. In 1977, he overcame the American Vitas Gerulaitis in a brilliant five set

"ONE OF MY DREAMS, WHEN I WAS A SMALL BOY, WAS TO PLAY AT THE CENTRE COURT. MY DREAM CAME TRUE..."
BJÖRN BORG

semi-final. In the final he survived in a five-setter against Jimmy Connors. In 1978 Borg made an awkward start in his opening match but proceeded dominantly to the final beating Connors again, this time quite easily. In 1979, the final also had the

champion against the ropes, before Borg beat Tanner in five sets.

In 1980 Borg had his notable confrontation with McEnroe in the final. It was among the best ever played at that stage. Borg won the final set by 8-6 to be champion for the fifth time. In 1981, though, McEnroe at last got his hands on the famous gold cup with a victory in four sets. For Borg it was virtually the end. Only 25, the years of intense effort had taken their toll. Later in 1981, he suddenly retired from the mainstream.

Idolised by young spectators and awesomely admired by all, Borg's legacy was immense. His example made the double-fisted backhand and patience an orthodoxy. His coolness under pressure, his speed about the court, his utter dependability from the back of the court through the use of heavy topspin, his fast reflexes on the volley, his formidable serve, his bloody-minded refusal to lose – all these attributes, honed to perfection by coach Lennart Bergelin – pointed the way forward. Björn Borg ranks as one of the giants of the game.

MARTINA NAVRATILOVA | 1978, 1979, 1982, 1983, 1984, 1985, 1986, 1987, 1990

THE STANDARD of women's play was taken to its highest level ever by Martina Navratilova, a brave left-handed serve and volleyer whose 349 career titles – 167 in singles, 173 in doubles and nine in mixed – make her the most successful tennis player of all time, male or female. Seven times she ended the year as the world's top-ranked player. She won a record nine singles titles on Wimbledon's Centre Court.

If Martina's greatest exploits were achieved as an American, her roots and training were entirely Czech. In 1975, as an 18-year old, she led Czechoslovakia to victory in the Federation Cup. Later that year, during the course of the US Open, she asked for refugee status.

Martina acquired her first Wimbledon title in 1976 with Chris Evert in the doubles, an event she later won with Billie Jean King and five times with Pam Shriver. Her breakthrough as singles champion came in 1978 when she survived a hard buffeting and won the final against Chris Evert. This was the first of Martina's five winning finals against her great American friend and rival. By the time of her third success against Evert in 1982, Martina was an American citizen. In 1983 Martina won the singles convincingly without losing a set, a feat she would repeat the following year and twice more – in 1986 and 1990. As her career unfolded, there was a feeling that we were witnessing the progress of the greatest champion of all time.

Yet still Martina had not equalled Billie Jean King's Wimbledon record of 20 titles. In the 1994 final, Spain's Conchita Martinez blunted Martina's attack and beat her in three sets. Announcing afterwards that she had played her last singles match, Martina seemed destined never to catch Billie Jean King. Yet, the following year she teamed with compatriot Jonathan Stark in the mixed to claim a 19th title. There followed a period when Martina had virtually retired.

In 2002 she returned to competition and got herself back to full fitness for 2003. In her 48th year, she teamed in the mixed doubles with Leander Paes. Martina rode an emotional wave all the way to her 20th title. The scenes on Centre Court as she hugged her partner were unforgettable. It was an appropriate postscript to a glorious career.

> "THIS IS WHAT I WANTED TO DO ALL MY LIFE. THIS IS WHERE I SHOULD BE"
> MARTINA NAVRATILOVA

‹ Martina Navratilova plucks some blades of Centre Court grass during an emotional farewell in 1994, her last singles final

Martina Navratilova in action in 1979 – her powerful left-handed attacking game set new standards in women's tennis ➤

JOHN McENROE | 1981, 1983, 1984

NO YOUNG PLAYER made so striking a debut at Wimbledon as this sharp left-handed New Yorker in the centenary year of 1977. It was as a junior, aged 18, that he came to Wimbledon primarily to compete in the junior tournament.

McEnroe was destined to bypass the juniors in a spectacular manner. He entered the qualifying competition, won his three rounds and thus came into The Championships proper. All notions of the junior event went by the board. For the first time in any major event a newcomer who was both a junior and a qualifier took himself to the heights of a semi-final. There he yielded to the weighty arts of Jimmy Connors but acquitted himself well in four close sets.

His high talents came fully to the fore in 1980, even if his Wimbledon climaxed in a loss. He reached the final when, gloriously, he won a fourth set in an 18-16 tiebreak and lost 6-8 in the fifth set to Björn Borg. By the end of 1980 McEnroe had twice won his own US Open title. Significantly, in the 1980 US final he beat Borg. It was in 1981 that McEnroe won his first Wimbledon singles. In the whole of this campaign he was never taken beyond four sets, not even in the final where he defeated Borg to

John McEnroe in 1984, flying high en route to his third singles title

John McEnroe serves during his 1981 winning final against Bjorn Borg, his first Wimbledon title ➤

end half a decade of the Swede's invincibility.

It was not only in his image as a great lawn tennis player, however, that McEnroe painted rich hues. His court misbehaviour led to an unprecedented step by the All England Club. Following his title success in 1981 they did not, as was the custom, elect him an honorary member of the Club.

> "I FELT A TINGLE DOWN MY SPINE… THERE'S NO OTHER TENNIS STAGE QUITE LIKE IT"
> JOHN McENROE

A year later McEnroe, though never looking as if he would emulate Little Lord Fauntleroy, retrieved his standing when the Club did give him the honour. Losing a stirring final in 1982 to Jimmy Connors, he re-established himself as champion a year later with a final victory over Chris Lewis.

McEnroe confirmed his standing as the best man in the world in the course of 1984, a year that included a crushing Wimbledon final victory over Jimmy Connors 6-1 6-1 6-2. The next year his biting power showed signs of lessening. Nonetheless, with three Wimbledon singles (and four doubles, three with Peter Fleming) and four US Opens on his record, his status among the all-time greats was assured.

BORIS BECKER | 1985, 1986, 1989

IN 1985 a German teenager made history by becoming the youngest man to win the Wimbledon singles title. Boris Becker was just 17 years 227 days old that sunny afternoon on Centre Court and his record is still intact. By beating South Africa's Kevin Curren in four sets, Boris also became the first non-seed and the first man from his country to wear the most prestigious crown in tennis.

From Becker's first-round win to his victory in the final, the tearaway teenager served like a demon. The headline writers had a field day: 'Boom Boom wins again'. The crowds warmed to the youngster's infectious enthusiasm. They roared their delight as he threw himself headlong, diving for wide volleys.

By successfully defending his title the following year against Ivan Lendl, Becker proved that he was a worthy champion. Five more finals on the Centre Court in the next nine years were further proof of his worth on grass. The first three were all against his great Swedish rival, Stefan Edberg, who beat him in 1988 and 1990, either side of Boris's third and last success in 1989. In 1991 Boris lost surprisingly to countryman Michael Stich in the first all-German final at Wimbledon and four years later he reached

the final for the last time and lost in four sets to Pete Sampras, the man who had succeeded him as the king of Centre Court.

Boris's three other Grand Slam wins came in 1989 in the US and 1991 and 1996 in Australia. Although Boris reached the semi-finals of the French Open three times, he could never find the consistency to win in Paris or, indeed, on clay generally.

Becker's attacking game, built around his serve, good volleys, a powerful backhand and great athleticism, brought him much success on fast surfaces, especially indoors. Three times in five years he led Germany to the final of the Davis Cup and twice to victory. Each time Sweden were the opponents.

After his retirement, a spell as German Davis Cup captain, charitable work on behalf of youngsters in Germany, and work as a television personality have kept Boris in the public eye and helped him to retain his enormous popularity.

> " IT'S AN EXPERIENCE WHERE
> ALL THE PLAYERS AGREE
> WITH ME – IT'S ONE OF
> A KIND "
> BORIS BECKER

◄ Boris Becker in typically spectacular diving action in 1993, with a game made for the fast grass of the Centre Court

Boris Becker became the youngest-ever men's singles champion with his victory in 1985 ➤

STEFFI GRAF | 1988, 1989, 1991, 1992, 1993, 1995, 1996

BORN NEAR Mannheim in Germany, not far from Boris Becker's birthplace of Leimen, Steffi Graf arrived at Wimbledon in 1984 shortly after her 15th birthday. The quiet, long-limbed young German was already a fine athlete with the build of a long-distance runner and a forehand that was lethal.

Fifteen years later she appeared on Centre Court for the last time, in her ninth singles final, established as the greatest woman player of her generation. With a career total of 22 Grand Slam singles titles to her name, Steffi was only two short of Margaret Court's record total of major wins. Eight times she ended the year as the world's no. 1. In terms of world rankings and prize money Steffi was without equal.

Graf's annus mirabilis was 1988. Her Grand Slam that year equalled the feats of Maureen Connolly (1953) and Margaret Court (1970) but, with tennis newly restored to the Olympic Games as a full medal sport, Steffi had the chance to make history. She took it brilliantly in Seoul by winning the gold medal to crown a year of achievement that may never be equalled.

Steffi's run of seven Wimbledon wins in

◄ Steffi Graf shares her moment of triumph with the fans, a ritual she performed seven times in nine years

⋏ A powerful overhead from Steffi Graf who rarely needed to come to the net

nine years began in 1988 with the first of two successive victories over Martina Navratilova, a win that reversed the result of the previous year's final. Her only other loss in a singles final came in 1999 against the powerful American Lindsay Davenport. In between, Steffi repulsed challenges from Gabriela Sabatini (1991), Monica Seles (1992), Jana Novotna (1993) and Arantxa Sanchez Vicario (1995 and 1996).

"THIS PLACE HAS GIVEN ME SO MANY MEMORIES AND INCREDIBLE MOMENTS"
STEFFI GRAF

Her capture of the 1995 US Open meant that she had won each of the four Grand Slam titles at least four times – another record which may never be broken.

A born competitor, Steffi had a ruthless will to win and was also blessed with outstanding powers of concentration. She had exceptional speed of foot, a supreme forehand, a first class serve and a penetrating sliced backhand that was used to set up chances for her winning forehand. Nor was Steffi a bad volleyer, but so dominant was she from the baseline that it was seldom necessary to advance to the net to win a point.

PETE SAMPRAS | 1993, 1994, 1995, 1997, 1998, 1999, 2000

ON WIMBLEDON'S Centre Court, Pete Sampras's record is unique. Seven times in eight years he made himself champion.

On fast courts, he was supreme. The Sampras serve was acknowledged as the world's best. The media christened him 'Pistol Pete'. But it was his second delivery that was so exceptional. Time after time in important matches, he would save break points with piercing deliveries that clipped the lines. He was utterly fearless. His other strengths included a fine volley, a wonderful running forehand, great athleticism, deceptive speed about the court and an indomitable will to win. As a serve-and-volley specialist, he had no equal.

His breakthrough year was 1990. At Wimbledon he had lost in the first round but two months later at the US Open, Sampras suddenly started to believe in himself. He powered his way to the title with wins over Ivan Lendl, John McEnroe and, in the final, Andre Agassi. At the age of 19, he had become the youngest man ever to win his national title. His great rivalry with Agassi became a central theme of the men's game in the 1990s.

Sampras was born in Washington DC of Greek parents who had emigrated to the USA. They were nervous spectators and present for only one of his Wimbledon finals when, in 2000 and ending in near darkness, he beat Pat Rafter in five sets to pass

⌃ Pete Sampras, the greatest grass-court player of his era

Sampras's powerful game made him virtually invincible on the Centre Court in the 1990s ➤

Roy Emerson's record of 12 major titles and secure his place in tennis history. As a tearful Pete scrambled up between the Centre Court spectators to embrace them in the stands, it was clear how much it had meant to them all. Previous Wimbledon final victims had been Jim Courier (1993), Goran Ivanisevic (1994), Boris Becker (1995), Cedric Pioline (1997), Ivanisevic again (1998) and Andre Agassi (1999).

The only trophy missing from his collection of silverware was a French Open title. Pete's attacking style was not suited to the slow clay in Paris and the closest he got to success in 13 appearances was a semi-final in 1996.

His 14 Grand Slams and seven Wimbledon titles were both records until his Grand Slam total was surpassed by Roger Federer in 2009. His prize money of over US$43 million was yet another record at the time. Sampras's place in the Pantheon of the very great tennis champions is assured.

VENUS WILLIAMS | 2000, 2001, 2005, 2007, 2008

THE STORY of Richard Williams and his tennis daughters reads more like a novel than an episode from real life.

An African-American, living in a tough part of Los Angeles, is watching tennis on television. Despite no experience, this ambitious man decides he will coach one of his daughters to stardom. His wife produces two more daughters for him: Venus and Serena, born 15 months apart. He purchases books and videos on coaching. He drills the girls mercilessly. They enter few junior tournaments. Stories circulate in the tennis world about this crazy American father. Whoever heard of a young player bypassing junior tennis and expecting to succeed?

We first saw Venus at Wimbledon in 1997. Her powerful forehands and double-handed backhands looked as if they would kill anything in their path. Just 17, she lost in the first round as she came to terms with a new surface. Later in the season, she smote her way to her first US Open final. Martina Hingis, three months younger than Venus but already the world no. 1, beat her in straight sets. There followed two years of consolidation, plus some frustration, as sister Serena beat her to a first Grand Slam title at the 1999 US Open.

Despite missing the first four months of the 2000 season with a wrist injury, Venus plundered

◄ Venus Williams on her way to her fourth title in 2007

◣ The moment of ecstasy after her victory in 2005

the silverware at Wimbledon. A difficult semi-final win over Serena was followed by a straight sets victory over fellow American Lindsay Davenport full of pace and power. Venus and Serena then combined to capture the first of their three doubles titles together over an eight-year period. Two months later Venus won her first US Open title and capped a tremendous year by taking the gold medal in singles and, with Serena, doubles at the Sydney Olympics. A year later she had retained her two Grand Slam titles. Justine Henin was her victim at Wimbledon and sister Serena at the US Open.

There followed three barren years as a succession of injuries and a growing interest in interior design shortened her opportunities to compete. It was at Wimbledon in 2005 that Venus announced her return to the world stage. Her final against Davenport throbbed with excitement before Venus squeaked home 9-7 in the final set.

Further wins in 2007 (over Marion Bartoli) and in 2008 (over sister Serena) confirmed Venus as one of the greatest women grass-court players since Martina Navratilova.

> **"IT'S SO REWARDING TO PERFORM HERE. I KNOW I HAVE THE CHANCE TO PLAY WELL AND MAKE HISTORY"**
> VENUS WILLIAMS

SERENA WILLIAMS | 2002, 2003, 2009

IT HAS NOT BEEN EASY. All her life Serena Williams has looked up to Venus as a role model.

Being the younger sister has brought psychological pressures that only siblings will understand. Beating her elder sister was simply not an option. Yet, as their tennis prowess grew under the stern eye of their father Richard, it became inevitable that the sisters would one day have to play each other in a major final.

Venus won their first three meetings comfortably. Then, in 1999, Serena surprised everyone by outhitting world no. 1, Martina Hingis, to claim the US Open title – a first for the Williams family. Two months later she surprised Venus by beating her in the final of the Grand Slam Cup. It was the psychological breakthrough she needed.

Two years later, after her career had been interrupted by a succession of frustrating injuries to knee and foot, Serena put together a remarkable run of successes. A victory over her sister in the 2002 French Open final was the first of four successive Grand Slam victories – all against Venus, including a two-set win at Wimbledon – that earned her a 'Serena Slam'. With another powerful performance against her sister in 2003, she successfully defended her Wimbledon crown, a win that earned her the no. 1 ranking for the first time.

After that golden spell, Serena experienced mixed fortunes on court as her off-court activities blossomed. She designed a clothing line, appeared in several TV dramas and sit-coms and became involved with charitable programmes that targeted at-risk youngsters. It was in 2005 that Serena resumed her winning ways at the Grand Slam

"I JUST WANTED TO WIN WIMBLEDON. I WANTED TO MAKE HISTORY"
SERENA WILLIAMS

level with a second title in Australia. A third and fourth would follow in 2007 and 2009. Meanwhile, she had added a third US Open title in 2008.

Serena gained her third Wimbledon crown in 2009 with yet another win against Venus. Together they also won a fourth doubles title. By claiming a 12th Grand Slam title in Australia in 2010 Serena proved again that, at her powerful best, she was still the finest woman player in the world. If she stays injury free and fully motivated, there is no reason why she should not add more. If she does, Venus will be the first to congratulate her.

◄ Serena Williams on her way to victory in 2009

Serena Williams celebrates winning her third title ➤

ROGER FEDERER | 2003, 2004, 2005, 2006, 2007, 2009

THE CAREER of Roger Federer is still unfinished, yet by the spring of 2010, still only 28, the Swiss superstar had already achieved tennis immortality.

His 15 Grand Slam titles, achieved in 2009 with a career-first French Open success followed by a sixth Wimbledon crown, surpassed the 14 won by Pete Sampras. The total became 16 in Australia in 2010. By reaching the final of all four Grand Slams in the same year three times and by winning Wimbledon and the US Open back-to-back four times in a row, Federer has set other records that may never be equalled. Until overtaken by Rafael Nadal in August 2008, Federer had been ranked no. 1 in the world for 237 consecutive weeks – another of those records.

There was early evidence that Roger had exceptional talent. In 1998, he won the junior singles and doubles titles at Wimbledon (only two others have done that). In 2001, now 19, he beat seven-times champion Pete Sampras in the fourth round. Two years later he joined Bjorn Borg, Pat Cash and Stefan Edberg as Wimbledon's only junior champions who have gone on to win the men's singles. His victories over Andy Roddick in the semi-finals and Mark Philippoussis in the final of the

2003 Championships now placed him at the top of the game.

Between 2004 and 2007, the confidence factor lifted Federer to new heights. His fifth consecutive win in 2007 equalled Bjorn Borg's record run achieved in the 1980s. His further Wimbledon victims were America's Andy Roddick (2004 and 2005) and Rafael Nadal of Spain (2006 and 2007).

A loss in five sets to the Spanish left-hander in the 2008 final provided one of the most dramatic matches ever seen on Centre Court. It ended in almost total darkness with Nadal prevailing 9-7 in the fifth set. The following year Roger, now married and about to become a father, regained his title. His third win over America's Andy Roddick in a Wimbledon final produced the longest-ever final set (16-14) in the history of The Championships. It also lifted him once again above Nadal to no.1 in the world rankings.

A natural athlete, Federer's speed of thought and movement, when allied to an abundant talent with the racket, give him options that others envy. Many consider that we have been witnessing the greatest striker of a tennis ball who ever lived. Perhaps his two finest weapons are his serve and his forehand. Both are hit with easy grace. Federer has reminded us all how beautiful this game can be.

> "EVERYTHING HERE, THE GREENNESS, THE GRASS, IS ALWAYS SPECIAL FOR ME."
> ROGER FEDERER

⬈ Roger Federer with an old friend after his victory against Rafael Nadal in 2007

Roger Federer in flying action with his trademark forehand ➤

It was a quarter-final between the 36-year-old Australian Ken Rosewall and the No. 1 American Cliff Richey. Rosewall, had already been in three Wimbledon finals and many expected him to make amends this year. But Richey had almost beaten him in Cincinnati the previous year, a 7-9 9-7 8-6 decision that augured well for this Wimbledon encounter. These two great athletes did not disappoint us.

Rosewall wins epic battle against Richey

The Financial Times

30th June 1971

By John Barrett

A near-veteran Australian and a young Texan of dynamic appeal lifted The Championships to new heights at Wimbledon yesterday. In the quarter-finals 36-year-old Ken Rosewall, the third seed, fought back with high courage after losing the first two sets to beat sixth-seeded Cliff Richey, 12 years his junior, in a nail-biting final set after being on court for a minute short of four hours.

Rosewall's clinging artistry, ragged at first but simply refusing to be denied, contrasted beautifully with the aggressive and purposeful play of the American to produce a match that will live alongside the other epics of the Centre Court.

The score of his win tells its own story. Sixty-four games of pulsating effort that were cruel in their demands upon the mental and physical reserves of both men. That Rosewall, at 36, can sustain an effort like this speaks volumes for his superb technique and unruffled acceptance of the terms of battle.

It was a match which nobody who witnessed it is likely to forget. It began quietly, like a small spark in some neglected corner of a great forest, caught alight with the brilliance of Richey's attack and the courage of Rosewall's recovery and was fanned into a roaring forest fire as the final set blazed to a fitting and emotional climax.

Rosewall began like a man with amnesia; he set up the openings but had forgotten what to do. In the first two sets Richey achieved his breaks at the right time and was ruthless in converting his lead. Surely, one felt, this must be the end for the brave Rosewall. Could a man his age expect to salvage the match from such a situation?

It was towards the end of the third set, at 5-4 to Rosewall I think, that the Australian, tidying up at the umpire's chair, stooped to pull up both of his socks. This symbolic gesture had a significance that was immediately apparent. He took advantage of a Richey double-fault to break for the set. Magic returned to Rosewall's racket. Unbelievably, after three hours and seven minutes they were level at two sets each.

So to the drama of the final set. At 4-4 Rosewall recovered from 15-40 to go 5-4 ahead and Richey served to save the match. Four times he was one point from defeat and four times saved himself with crowding volley and leaping smash.

This was raw courage. Both men were at the extremes of exhaustion and the tougher character would win. In the twelfth game Rosewall, now 6-5 ahead after recovering again from 15-40, forced a fifth match point with a forehand volley punched out of reach. A final backhand winner down the line saw him home and the stands erupted. For a full minute they stood and cheered as the little man, as humble in victory as he always has been in defeat, shyly acknowledged the acclaim.

4	6	6
6	3	4

The women's semi final between Evonne Goolagong and Chris Evert enriched the Wimbledon scene. Evonne was the defending holder and Chris was there for the first time. Their ages were 20 and 17 respectively. It was the match up all eagerly awaited.

MISS GOOLAGONG DEFIES A RICH CHALLENGE

The Guardian
6th July 1972
By David Gray

Goolagong v Evert at last and a victory for the champion by 4-6 6-3 6-4. There was a sense that history was being made at Wimbledon yesterday. The best players of the new generation were meeting for the first time, and the whole world was intrigued by the contest. And the beautiful part of it was that expectation was totally fulfilled.

There could hardly have been a semi-final full of higher excitement or deeper emotion. The tennis had been brave, skilful, dramatic, and full of style, fluctuation and contrast. It was chivalrously won and graciously lost. There could not have been a better advertisement for the new order in the game. The players had stretched their store of talent and energy to the utmost. Everything had been given. Devastating returns had been countered by seemingly impossible winners, and the rallies had become anthologies of great shots.

There is a special magic about matches full of positive groundstrokes, and this was a contest to remember and cherish. 'Like Connolly v Hart', said a French friend at the end, and it was impossible to think of higher praise.

Miss Goolagong won because once again she responded to danger by hitting with increasing pace and discipline. Danger stimulated her. This was the victim who didn't give in. Miss Goolagong may have begun untidily, presenting her points with a profligacy which is not usually expected from Wimbledon champions. But she won the match from a set and 0-3 down, and in the crises in the second and third sets she scarcely wasted a point.

From 0-3 Miss Goolagong won seven successive games. She looked like a champion again. Suddenly she had woken. Then she lost a service game to be down 1-2 in the third set, but broke back at once. The exchange of services was repeated again immediately. Miss Evert may have lost the initiative, but she was hanging on desperately. All the time, however, Miss Goolagong was playing with greater audacity and authority.

Miss Evert held on in a long game for 4-4, with Miss Goolagong mounting a full scale attack. But the next time she served, the pressure proved too much. Miss Goolagong was in full cry. The bombardment became fiercer, and the champion became more ambitious and more successful. A drop shot, a forehand which dipped over the net, an American error, and one last wonderful volley settled the matter. It could not really have been a better match.

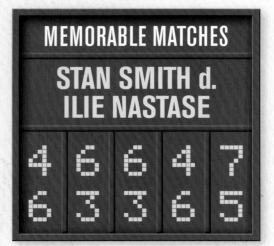

4 6 6 4 7
6 3 3 6 5

The big corporal outguns Nastase in wonderful climax
Stan's armoury wins it

Would 1972 be the year for the supremely gifted Ilie Nastase? Or would the losing finalist the previous year, the 6 feet 4 inches tall, straight backed Stan Smith of the US Army prevail? The first final to be played on a Sunday, due to rain, proved to be a thriller.

Daily Mail
10th July 1972
by Laurie Pignon

Wimbledon opened its gates on a Sunday, and our eyes to a new tennis world, when Corporal Stanley Roger Smith of the United States Army defeated Ilie Nastase, of Rumania, 4-6, 6-3, 6-3, 4-6, 7-5 in a match which can be argued by old men as the greatest final ever played.

For two hours, 43 minutes, these two, who differ in almost everything but the colour of their skin, shared the same torments of ambition and the same fears.

They suffered... and how they must have suffered, as classic shots, worthy of winners, came back again and yet again, making almost impossible demands on mind and muscle. You couldn't tell where genius ended and instinct took over.

Until this match, Smith, a blond giant of 6ft. 4in., was grossly under-rated.

Yesterday, against a world master of stroke play, Smith proved that he can produce every shot in the book.

Hundred mile an hour screamers, which bought up dust from the crumbling court, were broken up with gentle stop volleys when the ball seemed to float over the net like a giant snowflake.

The test for Smith came in the fifth game of the fifth set, which went to seven deuces before he was able to hold his service with a stop volley that seemed to melt into the ground.

The Rumanian, desperately snatching at half chances, saved three match points. At the fourth Smith, under pressure, put up a short lob which was awkwardly placed over Nastase's backhand shoulder. He made the shot which he had done successfully a dozen times before. But now, when he needed it most, it folded on him and the ball fell into the net.

It was like a curtain falling at the end of a great opera.

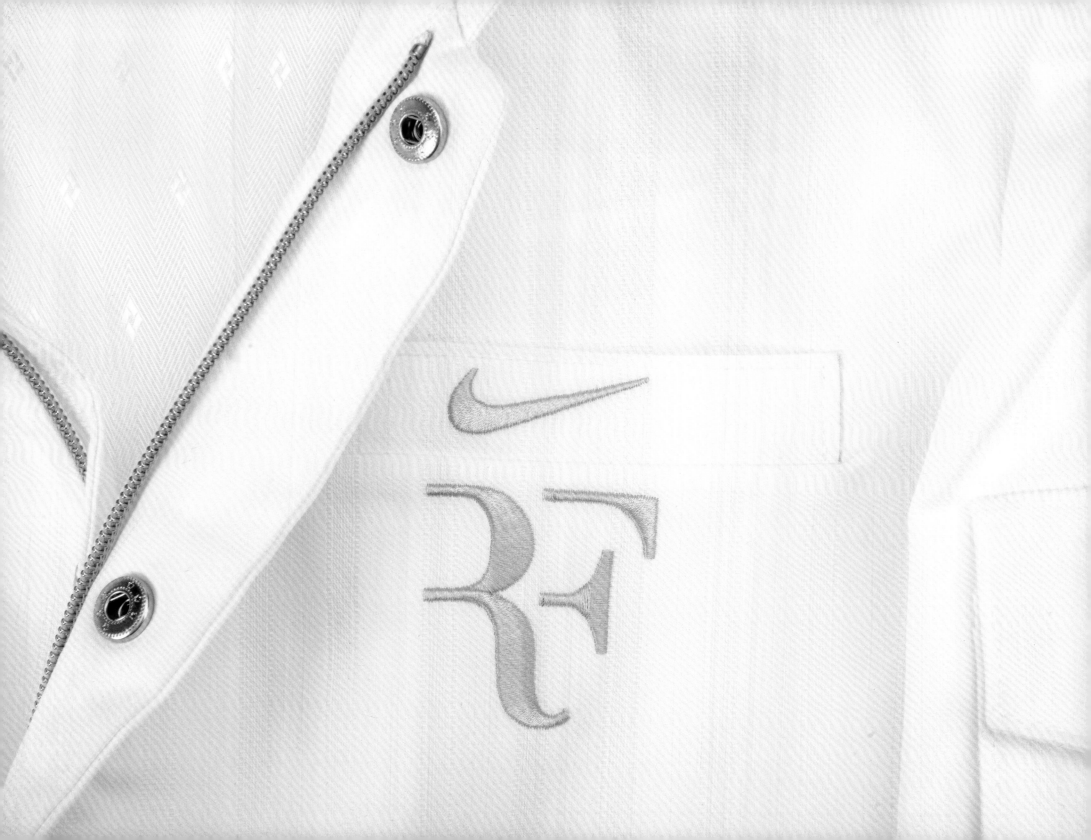

CENTRE COURT TREASURES

THE AWARD-WINNING state-of-the-art Wimbledon Lawn Tennis Museum features many exhibits and artefacts celebrating The Championships and the Centre Court experience. Here are just a few of them.

Exhibits range from archive recordings of matches and champions to visual displays and mementos which illustrate the history of The Championships including the fashions, the rackets and the trophies. The cinema features a 200° screen immersing the viewer into a film, shot from five cameras on the Centre Court, illustrating the science of tennis. Another exhibit recreates the 1980s men's dressing room while a ghost-like image of John McEnroe reminisces about great players and rivalries.

"*I guess I should have known,*" said McEnroe. "*Yet when I first walked around the winding corridors of the Wimbledon Lawn Tennis Museum, it still came as a surprise to discover such a diverse collection of paintings, photographs, rackets, clothing and general memorabilia… the Museum has so much to offer.*"

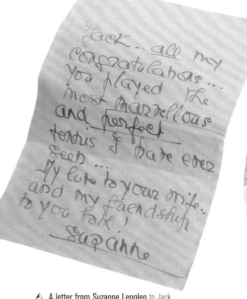

⬈ **A letter from Suzanne Lenglen** to Jack Crawford following the Australian's win over the holder, Ellsworth Vines, in 1933

⬊ **John McEnroe's ghost-like presentation** is the highlight for many visitors to the Museum

⬋ **Fred Perry's Slazenger All-White**, a model introduced by the company during Perry's winning run at the 1934 Australian Championships and used by the British no. 1 thereafter

A box of Slazenger hand-stitched tennis balls, individually wrapped, as used at the first Championships at the new ground in 1922

A book of Centre Court tickets from 1947, plus individual tickets from 1949 and 1961 ➤

Angela Mortimer's Dunlop Maxply racket used to win the 1961 Championship and her trademark shirt and shorts ➤

Rod Laver's trusty Dunlop Maxply, the model used by the Australian in winning all four of his singles titles ➤

⅄ Chris Evert's Converse tennis shoes and Ellesse socks

The Wilson T 2000 used by Billie Jean King in 1970 ➤

⬈ The dress and pink cardigan worn by Virginia Wade during her winning final against Betty Stove in the Queen's Silver Jubilee year, 1977

Bjorn Borg's Fila shirt and shorts, plus the famous headband worn by the great Swede during his memorable winning final against John McEnroe in 1980

The Dunlop Max 200G, an injection moulded graphite racket used by John McEnroe to win his 1983 and '84 titles. In 1981 he had won using a wooden McEnroe Maxply and is the only player to have won the men's singles title using both wood and graphite

John McEnroe's Nike tennis shoes worn by the American in 1985

The Wilson T 2000 used by Jimmy Connors in 1977, the same model he used in his two winning years, 1974 and 1982 ➤

Bjorn Borg's wooden Donnay racket, the model he used in all five of his Championship wins ➤

The distinctive outfit worn by Martina Navratilova during her winning final against Zina Garrison in 1990

Boris Becker's Puma tennis shoes worn during his second winning final, against Ivan Lendl, in 1986

The Head racket used by Andre Agassi in 1994

One of the trademark headbands worn by the 1987 champion Pat Cash which were always thrown to the spectators after his matches

The dress worn by Maria Sharapova when she beat Serena Williams in the 2004 final to claim a first Wimbledon title as a 17-year-old

The Nike shoes of seven-times men's singles champion Pete Sampras, autographed by the great man

◣ **The cardigan** worn by Roger Federer in 2008

Rafael Nadal's racket and outfit from the same year, 2008, when he triumphed at Wimbledon for the first time ◥ ➤

◣ **Roger Federer's cap** which he and his team wore in 2008

◣ **The Reebok shoes** worn by Venus Williams during her 2001 final against Justine Henin that earned her a second title

◁ **New treasures in the Museum** include Roger Federer's military style jacket, shoes and headband from his record-breaking 15th Grand Slam title victory in 2009

◁ **The dress worn by Venus Williams** in the 2009 final which she lost to her sister, Serena

The shoes worn by Serena Williams in 2009 when she added to her previous victories in 2002 and 2003 ➤

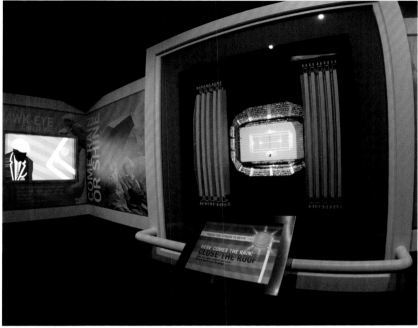

ROOM WITH A VIEW

The real treasure, though, as always is the Centre Court itself. A fresh, innovative viewing platform, known as *CentreCourt 360*, has now opened and brings a visit to the Museum to a new level. Visitors can come closer than ever before, only steps away from the famous grass, and enjoy an up close view of the court from the eyes of a spectator. Interactive touch screens add to the experience by highlighting features of the historic venue and its new retractable roof.

Jimmy Connors, the holder, was the overwhelming favourite against his fellow American, Arthur Ashe, in the 1975 final. The contest, a battle of power and tactical awareness, became one of the most intriguing and extraordinary of modern times.

King Arthur holds court

The Observer

6th July 1975

By Christopher and Shirley Brasher

Executioners, never wavering as they brought their sharp axes down on their opponents' heads, have won the 1975 Wimbledon championships. Yesterday, it was Arthur Ashe who, like Billie Jean King on Friday, wielded his axe with unerring tactical sense – an axe which he had weighted with experience and the confidence of a thorough preparation.

And yet who would have expected that the 31-year-old American – the first black athlete to appear in the men's final – would upset the odds so dramatically. Connors was 7-1 on to win and yet it was Ashe who took the title 6-1 6-1 5-7 6-4.

Those first two sets were the biggest upset in the history of Wimbledon finals. Ashe played tennis of which dreams are made.

Ashe had thought deeply about the match. First, his service: his first service had to be constantly changed in pace and direction. Next, he must never give Connors any pace – never give Connors the chance to blast fast balls back even faster. Then he must always vary his spin, again so that Connors could never settle and play his particular firebrand tennis. In short, he dictated the terms, the framework of the match; it was like watching a king being publicly deposed. Surely it would never reach the final point of execution?

In the third set, Connors began to get the range with his powerful weapons. He was into the match, his shattered confidence restored. Games went with service to four-all in the fourth set. Fifteen-forty to Ashe and the crowd could see the axe on Connors' neck. Ashe returned Connors' service to his feet and all that remained was for Ashe to serve for the championship.

He sat on the chair, eyes closed, relaxed, composing himself, thinking, he said, of nothing. He needed only one match point – an acutely angled first service, a scrambled high return from Connors, and the crowd were on their feet cheering before Ashe even had a chance to smash the ball away. That was it – not a great match but a memorable final.

BJORN BORG d. VITAS GERULAITIS

6	3	6	3	8
4	6	3	6	6

The 1977 semi-final pitched the existing champion Bjorn Borg against his friend and regular practice partner, America's Vitas Gerulaitis, who was seeking his first win against the popular Swede. It produced one of those classic encounters whose outcome was in doubt until the last ball.

Three hours of summer lightning

The Times

1st July 1977

By Rex Bellamy

Bjorn Borg's 6-4 3-6 6-3 3-6 8-6 win over Vitas Gerulaitis in three hours and four minutes was a Wimbledon classic.

In the fifth set, Gerulaitis had a point for a 4-2 lead but stayed back on his service and when he eventually charged to the net, was off the mark with a forehand volley. Both men later agreed that this point was critical. Borg broke back for 3-3 instead of going 2-4 down.

In the 11th game, Borg, serving, three times, heard the umpire call "deuce". Again, the champion was teetering on the brink of a plunge to oblivion. But three games later, somehow mustering his drained resources for a huge effort, he set about Gerulaitis's service and broke through for the match.

Beauty should be enjoyed not measured. But how to describe this sample, save in terms of three dazzling hours of summer lightning? During matches such as this, grass court tennis achieves a splendour that cannot be surpassed.

A reasonable man would not think it possible for two tennis players to maintain such precision at such high speed under such pressure over such a long period. The sustained quickness of footwork, reactions, and racket control was astonishing. They gave us plenty of variety: drops and lobs, sudden changes of pace and angle, to punctuate all the whirling, pounding agility and aggression. At times the geometry they created almost happened too fast to be properly savoured; the entire match was dominated by earned points.

This was a perfect example of grasscourt tennis at its best.

There were emotional scenes on the Centre Court in 1977 as Virginia Wade sought to become a third post–war British ladies' winner – before the Queen in her Silver Jubilee Year and in the year of Wimbledon's centenary.

The Times

2nd July 1977

By Rex Bellamy

"It was so wonderful to have the Queen there. The crowd cheering for her and cheering for me. The Duchess of Kent waving. All the singing. It was so friendly. Just like a fairy tale." Virginia Wade was bubbling over.

They were inevitably emotional scenes on Wimbledon's Centre Court after her 4-6, 6-3, 6-1 win over Betty Stove, in the women's singles final, which lasted an hour and 38 minutes. The emotion sprang partly from patriotism, partly from the public's recognition of a player who, at the age of 31, had become champion at the sixteenth attempt.

After the Queen's appearance and the National Anthem, the players appeared. Union Jacks, large and small, were evident everywhere. Miss Stove may reasonably have suspected that were she

Wimbledon acclaims Miss Wade

to beat Miss Wade in such an environment, she would be sent to the Tower if not worse.

The first set, though, was dominated by Miss Stove's imposing physique and lazily explosive shots. It was time for Miss Wade to take a more positive role in the match; to enforce errors rather than hope for them. She had to make Miss Stove dash about.

This Miss Wade did. In the second set the crowd became noisier through relief, and the beginnings of excitement – as she went to 3-0 and had points for 4-0 and 4-1. Miss Stove came back to 3-3. But the next game was perhaps the most decisive of the match. Miss Wade had all the crashing, pounding fury of a mountain stream following a well defined course as she held her service for 4-3.

Miss Stove was done for. She had not been able to play her best tennis long enough. From 0-4 down she rescued one game from the wreckage of the third set but no more. The match ended with a forehand return too good for her lunging racket to control.

What a roar there was, what a raging sea of hands. A minute passed before the umpire, dutifully observing the last rites, could announce the score. Then the Queen came on court – the monarch of a realm greeting the monarch of a sport. Flags waved everywhere.

There was a spontaneous chorus of "For she's a jolly good fellow" (or was it, more aptly — "For she's a jolly good player"?). Hurrahs rang around the Centre Court.

THE ROYAL BOX

THE ROYAL BOX has always been a focal point in the theatre of the Centre Court. There has been a Royal Box at the south end of the Centre Court since the opening of the new grounds in 1922. At the old grounds at Worple Road a Royal Box did not exist; when royalty attended, the Committee Box was suitably converted for the occasion.

The Royal Box, which seats 74 people (in dark green Lloyd Loom wicker chairs), is used for the entertainment of guests from the Royal Family and from the tennis world, including supporters of British tennis, as well as prominent individuals from other walks of life. Invitations come from the Chairman of the Club on behalf of the Committee of Management. Guests are invited to lunch, tea and drinks at the end of the day, which take place within the Clubhouse.

"DRESS IS SMART, LOUNGE SUITS/ JACKET AND TIE ETC. LADIES ARE ASKED NOT TO WEAR HATS AS THEY TEND TO OBSCURE THE VISION OF THOSE SEATED BEHIND THEM."
OFFICIAL GUIDANCE FOR ROYAL BOX GUESTS

⅄ The Royal Box awaits its front row guests | ⅄ The French polisher at work on the eve of The Championships | ➢ Queen Mary in the front row of the Royal Box during the 1922 Championships

King George V and Queen Mary were regular visitors to The Championships. Here, in 1933, they are seated either side of the King of Spain

ROYAL GUESTS

King George V and Queen Mary were avid spectators at The Championships, being present most years from 1919 to 1934. When King George V, accompanied by Queen Mary, opened the Church Road ground and the new Centre Court in 1922, also present were the Prince of Wales (later King Edward VIII) and Prince Albert (later King George VI).

Queen Mary continued this association after the King's death and from 1935 to 1951 missed only the meeting of 1936. Queen Elizabeth II has visited The Championships three times. In 1957 she presented Althea Gibson with the singles trophy on court. She did the same in 1962 when Rod Laver won the second of his four singles titles. In 1977, the year of her Silver Jubilee, Her Majesty witnessed Virginia Wade's emotional win over Betty Stove before presenting her with her trophy.

The arrival of the Queen in 1957 for her first visit to The Championships

Members of the Kent family have occupied the office of President of the All England Lawn Tennis & Croquet Club continuously since 1929. Following the wartime death of the Duke in 1942, his wife acted as President for over 25 years — first as the Duchess of Kent and from 1961 as Princess Marina. Since 1969 the

A youthful Princess Anne arriving for an afternoon in the Royal Box

(middle) Princess Diana and the Duke of Kent on men's finals day in 1995

Rafael Nadal, the first champion to climb to the Royal Box, thanks Crown Prince Felipe of Spain for his support after his victory in 2008

present Duke of Kent has carried out his duties as President with great enthusiasm.

Princess Anne has also attended The Championships, including in 1969 when, appropriately, she presented the ladies' trophy to Britain's Ann Jones. Princess Diana was also a frequent and enthusiastic visitor. The Duke of York attended in 2008. Other regular Royal visitors in recent years have included Prince and Princess Michael of Kent and the Duchess of Gloucester, the Honorary President of the LTA.

Bowing or curtseying by players to Royalty and the Royal Box, as they entered and left the Centre Court, used to be a familiar part of the traditional etiquette. In

2003, however, the Duke of Kent requested players not to bow or curtsey except when the Queen or the Prince of Wales was present.

Royal Box guests have frequently included royalty and heads of state from other countries. In 2008, Crown Prince Felipe of Spain was present to see the victory of Rafael Nadal — and able to offer his congratulations to his countryman in the Royal Box itself after Nadal's climb.

"*On one occasion in the 1950s, a Committee member was making polite conversation to an African monarch, who had been given into his care after a request from the then Foreign Service. As the King, who had said nothing all afternoon, was rising to leave, the Committee member asked him what his impressions had been, to which came the reply 'Yes, thank you. I have enjoyed myself here at Henley.'*"

(Recounted in '*Wimbledon: Centre Court of the Game*' by Max Robertson)

OTHER GUESTS

Guests in the Royal Box have, over the years, included politicians and statesmen/women of a variety of hues. British Prime Ministers during the last fifty years who have attended include Harold Wilson, Edward Heath, Margaret Thatcher and John Major.

Spectators often keep a keen and watchful eye for other 'celebrities' from stage, screen or other walks of life. On the tennis front, past Wimbledon champions are always welcome guests and many are attendees, particularly on the two finals days. The presence in 2009 of Pete Sampras was particularly appropriate to witness Roger Federer's achievement in surpassing his record with a 15th Grand Slam singles title.

The Duchess of Gloucester, Honorary President of the LTA, leads the applause in 2006 on the first Saturday when sporting and showbiz personalities were guests in the Royal Box

It has become customary, on the first Saturday, for guests to include a number of sporting stars and past tennis favourites. A moving moment for many was in 2006. On the first Saturday, five Wimbledon ladies' singles champions — Maria Bueno, Margaret Court, Billie-Jean King, Martina Navratilova and Steffi Graf — were introduced to the crowd (see picture, above right). Between them, they had won 28 Wimbledon singles titles and a total 202 Grand Slam titles in singles, doubles and mixed. Each was presented with an inscribed Waterford crystal bowl by the Duchess of Gloucester, Honorary President of the LTA.

Five of Wimbledon's greatest lady champions (from left to right): Martina Navratilova, Billie Jean King, Steffi Graf, Margaret Court and Maria Bueno, were honoured guests in 2006

For all guests, a day in the Royal Box is a special and memorable occasion, as this extract from a piece in *The Daily Telegraph* by Boris Johnson, Mayor of London, who attended on men's final day in 2008, poetically illustrates:

> "I had never been to Wimbledon before, and I discovered that it is just about the sublimest thing this country has to offer. Oh it wasn't just the flummery of the Royal Box, though I must say that the quality of the entertainment was stratospheric. It was the game that was the thing. It was the theatre. It was a pageant that told you all you needed to know about the human condition.
>
> As the evening wore on, the passions rose. The crowd started to gasp at every point like a huge vacuum cleaner. The shades lengthened, and the pigeons started to swoop across the court as though they had no idea of the titanic battle taking place.
>
> It was just magic, and it struck me that it could not happen anywhere else but the Centre Court at Wimbledon. I feel grateful beyond words to have been there."

Mighty Martina
The no-where girl is queen of Wimbledon

The signs had been apparent for some time. Martina Navratilova, the powerful left-hander from Czechoslovakia, who had defected to the United States in 1975, was beginning to fulfil her enormous potential. But was she yet good enough to outwit the smartest of recent champions, her friend from America, Chris Evert? Their cliff-hanger of a final in 1978 provided the answer.

Daily Mail

8th July 1978

By Laurie Pignon

Martina Navratilova, the girl without a country, became queen of Wimbledon yesterday when she beat Chris Evert 2-6 6-4 7-5. The stateless Czech had rehearsed in her mind how she would feel should her dearest tennis ambition come true.

When it did, all she could say at her moment of triumph was: "I feel so many emotions I don't know which one I should feel first."

Perhaps it was because she was afraid of remembering the utter loneliness she felt on the Centre Court when, during a break in play, she looked longingly into the sea of faces wishing with all her heart that her parents and sister and even the puppy she left behind in Prague were among them.

The faint hope that winning something as big as Wimbledon might make the Czech government forgive if not forget her defection to the United States and allow her to meet her family, was a giant incentive on the way to the top. Afterwards she said: 'Whatever my citizenship papers say deep down in my heart I will always be a Czech'.

Two weeks ago in Eastbourne Miss Navratilova defeated Miss Evert in three

sets after the American had held one match point. Yesterday, Miss Evert got no closer than serving for a 5-2 lead which did not materialise in the final set. Miss Navratilova, formerly of Prague, now living in Dallas, dropped only one point in the last three games.

The spirit in which the match was played was as impeccable as one would expect from the two top women of the world who are the best of friends. The match must rank among the top dozen women's finals since the war, with innumerable changes of fortune in its 102 minutes.

When it was over Martina held the champion's gold plate above her head with pride but I fancy she would have exchanged it at that moment for something like a fatherly hug.

MEMORABLE MATCHES
BJORN BORG d. JOHN McENROE

1	7	6	6	8
6	5	3	7	6

Bjorn Borg's rivalry with John McEnroe produced some glorious matches, none greater than the epic three hour 53 minutes final of 1980. Borg was seeking a record fifth title. This was McEnroe's first final. The fourth set tie-break, 20 minutes of 34 pulsating points, produced some of the finest shot-making ever seen on the Centre Court and stretched the nerves of the spectators almost to breaking point.

Borg and the loser who took all but his title

The Times

7th July 1980

By Rex Bellamy

The Wimbledon Championships could hardly have finished in greater splendour. The men's singles final was a marvellous match: one of the most exciting there has ever been and, for the most of is duration, astonishing in its sustained quality. An hour and 17 minutes after having reached the first of his eight match points, Bjorn Borg beat John McEnroe 1-6 7-5 6-3 6-7 8-6. It was Borg's longest and most arduous final. We shall long remember the brilliant treasures these two shared with us.

There were two phases when it seemed McEnroe might take charge. Having won the first set, he had three break points when Borg was serving at 4-4 in the second. With a sudden surge of authority, Borg won five successive games. At the first sniff of a chance he broke through.

McEnroe's other chance came at the beginning of the fifth set. Borg was feeling low because seven match points had drifted away – two at 5-4 and the rest in the tie-break. Four had been on Borg's own service. In the first game of the fifth set McEnroe hit two winners to reduce Borg to 0-30. But Borg's response was to win 28 of his remaining 29 service points. Considering the quality of McEnroe's returns – and the length of time they had been punishing their bodies – this was probably the most amazing and critical serving performance of Borg's career.

McEnroe had the better touch and the more flexible command of spin. He was so quick to the net – and at the net – that even Borg's passing shots never really fired until the third set, in which Borg seemed to grow bigger and stronger and faster as confidence flooded into him for the first time. Borg's ground-strokes were the sounder and often the more powerful or deceptive. But there was nothing between the two men except experience.

In the fourth set tiebreak greatness descended on the match. The players' ground strokes were so fierce that, as each in turn flung himself in vain at passing shots, Borg tumbled head over heels and two points later McEnroe went flat on his face. This was violently exciting tennis in which each man made terrible demands on heart and muscles and sinews. The speed of shots and reactions, racket-handling and timing were breathtaking.

McEnroe had been booed on to the court. At the end he was given a standing ovation – because he had played like a man and behaved like a man. He had lost a tennis match, but in terms of public acclaim he had won Wimbledon. As for Borg, for the third time he is in sight of a grand slam. Next stop, New York.

GREAT DOUBLES PAIRS

⋏ "Toto" Brugnon and Henri Cochet

IT IS NOT ONLY singles matches that have enthralled the Centre Court crowds. For many, the excitement of sharp rallies, angles not seen in singles, the cut-and-thrust of volleying exchanges, as well as astonishing defence with pairs working skilfully together, have provided some of the most enjoyable and entertaining tennis at Wimbledon, whether in men's, ladies' or mixed doubles.

For many years all the great singles players would also compete in the doubles events. Three men and five ladies have even carried off all three titles in the same year, but that spectacular feat has not been achieved since 1973. The pressure of achieving success in singles, plus the greater depth of talent in both the men's and ladies' game, has meant that fewer of the leading singles players now step onto the doubles stage.

Here we acknowledge the great doubles players who have won three or more men's or ladies' doubles titles at Wimbledon. These achievements have almost invariably been completed on the Centre Court, the court of champions. Since 1922, 13 men and 16 women have achieved that feat at Wimbledon – not always with the same partner. Five men's pairs and seven ladies' pairs stand alone as having triumphed together on three or more occasions.

MEN

JEAN BOROTRA /JACQUES BRUGNON (1932 & 1933)
BOROTRA /RENE LACOSTE (1925).
BRUGNON/HENRI COCHET (1926 & 1927)

Of the four French 'Musketeers' it was Jacques 'Toto' Brugnon who was the doubles expert. Twice with Jean Borotra and twice with Henri Cochet he claimed the Wimbledon title, besides winning the French Championships five times and the Australian Championships once. He also contributed 22 Davis Cup doubles wins from the 31 ties in which he participated.

FRANK SEDGMAN/KEN McGREGOR (1951 & 1952)
SEDGMAN/JOHN BROMWICH (1948)

The first of the great Australian pairs of the "post-war" years was Frank Sedgman and Ken McGregor whose consecutive titles in 1951 and '52 revealed a wonderful combination of power and athleticism. The young Sedgman had first won in 1948 with the veteran John Bromwich whose legendary partnership with Adrian Quist had brought them eight Australian titles together between 1938 and 1950, the year they won together at Wimbledon.

Frank Sedgman and Ken McGregor, the first of the great post-War Australian pairs ➤

LEW HOAD/KEN ROSEWALL (1953 & 1956)
HOAD/REX HARTWIG (1955)

Australia's teenage tennis 'twins', Lew Hoad and Ken Rosewall, burst on to the world scene in 1953. They won the first of their two Wimbledon titles together that year at the age of 18, one month after their first major success in Paris. They offered a superb combination of power and artistry. It was clear they would have outstanding careers. In 1956 they won a second title together and then added the US title to their growing collection before turning professional. It was Hoad's third success because, in between, he had collected the 1955 title with Rex Hartwig.

ROY EMERSON/NEALE FRASER (1959 & 1961)
EMERSON/ROD LAVER (1971)

With the departure of Rod Laver to the pro ranks in 1962, his fellow Australian Roy Emerson dominated the men's game for the next five years. Altogether he collected a record 28 Grand Slam titles, 12 in singles and 16 in doubles. Three of the latter were at Wimbledon, two with Neale Fraser and one with Laver himself. In France Emerson won the men's doubles title six years in a row with five different partners – a remarkable achievement.

BOB HEWITT/FREW MCMILLAN (1967, 1972 & 1978)
HEWITT/FRED STOLLE (1962 & 1964)

Bob Hewitt, whose partnership with Fred Stolle yielded two titles each in Australia and at Wimbledon, left Australia for South Africa after a dispute with his national Association and started to represent his new country in 1967. With his South African partner Frew McMillan he carved out a second career, winning three Wimbledon titles, plus one each in France and America, as well as six titles at home in South Africa. Both men were delightful artists of the doubles court, masters of all the angles, and expert mixed doubles players. Hewitt won six Grand Slam mixed titles with four different partners while McMillan won four with two partners.

JOHN NEWCOMBE/TONY ROCHE (1965, 1968, 1969, 1970 & 1974)
NEWCOMBE/ KEN FLETCHER (1966)

The powerful combination of the right-handed John Newcombe and the left-handed Tony Roche proved irresistible in the late 1960s and early '70s. Both fine singles players, together they formed one of the great doubles teams. They won five Wimbledon titles (then a modern record among men), four in Australia, three in America and one in France. Individually they enjoyed further successes at the Grand Slams with other partners and in the Davis Cup they contributed to two Challenge Round successes against Spain.

⌃ The "Woodies", Todd Woodbridge (left) and Mark Woodforde

PETER FLEMING/JOHN McENROE (1979, 1981, 1983 & 1984)
McENROE/MICHAEL STICH (1992)

Peter Fleming once graciously said, "*The best doubles team in the world is John McEnroe and anyone*". This self-deprecating remark concealed his own considerable contribution to one of the greatest doubles teams of modern times. Together they won four of the five Wimbledon finals they contested and won the US Open three times as well as seven consecutive Masters crowns. Their Davis Cup record of 14 wins from 15 matches played is the finest in modern times. Fleming's dependable right-court returns provided the perfect platform for McEnroe's quick-silver interceptions and explosive smashes which thrilled the crowd.

TODD WOODBRIDGE/MARK WOODFORDE (1993, 1994, 1995, 1996, 1997 & 2000)
TODD WOODBRIDGE/ JONAS BJORKMAN (2002, 2003 & 2004)

In the modern age of doubles specialists no pair could match the record of the all-conquering 'Woodies'. Todd Woodbridge and the left-handed Mark Woodforde won five Wimbledons in a row and then, in centenary year, added a sixth. With the retirement of Woodforde after the Aussies had completed a career doubles Grand Slam and won the silver medal at the Sydney Olympics, Woodbridge formed a new partnership with Sweden's Jonas Bjorkman. Together they won three times in a row at Wimbledon from 2002 and Woodbridge ended his career with 83 men's doubles titles, an open era record.

LOUISE BROUGH/ MARGARET OSBORNE DU PONT (1946, 1948, 1949, 1950 & 1954)

Outstandingly the greatest American doubles team of the immediate post-war era, Louise Brough and Margaret Osborne du Pont won the Wimbledon title five times in nine years and totally dominated their own US Championships, winning 12 times between 1942 and 1957. In addition they triumphed in Paris on three occasions. They never travelled together to Australia. Both were wonderful servers, powerful volleyers and both returned consistently. Her doubles skill enabled Louise Brough, one of sport's finest female athletes, to win all three titles twice at Wimbledon — in 1948 and 1950.

LADIES

mixed which remains a record for doubles events at The Championships.

HELEN WILLS MOODY/ELIZABETH RYAN (1927 & 1930)
WILLS-MOODY/HAZEL WIGHTMAN (1924)

Virtually unbeatable in singles, America's great pre-war champion Helen Wills could also play good doubles when she put her mind to it. For the first of her three titles she had as her partner one of the game's greatest benefactors, Hazel Wightman who later donated a Cup for annual competition between the women of America and Great Britain. For her second and third titles Helen played with Elizabeth Ryan.

SUZANNE LENGLEN/ELIZABETH RYAN (1919, 1920, 1921, 1922, 1923 & 1925)
RYAN/AGATHA MORTON (1914), MARY K. BROWNE (1926), HELEN WILLS (1927 & 1930) & SIMONE MATHIEU (1933 & 1934)

Suzanne Lenglen was equally as good at doubles as she was on the singles court. With her American partner Elizabeth Ryan she won six times before retiring from the game during the 1926 Championships. The indefatigable Elizabeth amassed a total of 19 Wimbledon titles, 12 in ladies' doubles and seven in

SHIRLEY FRY/DORIS HART (1951, 1952 & 1953)
HART/PAT TODD (1947)

It was the misfortune of Shirley Fry and Doris Hart that their careers coincided with those of Louise Brough and Margaret Osborne du Pont. In any other era these two great champions would have won more than the three consecutive doubles titles they claimed at Wimbledon between 1951 and 1953. Those same years they also won their own US Championships and then went one better by adding a fourth American title in 1954.

MARTINA NAVRATILOVA/PAM SHRIVER (1981, 1982, 1983, 1984 & 1986)
NAVRATILOVA /CHRIS EVERT (1976) & BILLIE JEAN KING (1979)

Steadily building her legend, in 1981 Martina Navratilova turned to Pam Shriver as a doubles partner. It became one of the game's great pairings. Shriver's right court returns and steady serve, allied to a long reach at the net, were the perfect foil for Navratilova's all round power and her expertise as a volleyer. Together they dominated the early 1980s, reaching six consecutive Wimbledon finals and walking off with the title on five occasions. During that same period they took six Australian titles together, four in France and four in America.

GIGI FERNANDEZ/NATASHA ZVEREVA (1992, 1993, 1994 & 1997)
ZVEREVA/LARISSA SAVCHENKO (1991)

Some pairs seem to click from the first time they play together. America's Gigi Fernandez, born in Puerto Rico, and her Ukrainian partner Natasha Zvereva were such a team. They exuded joy and confidence and always seemed to be smiling. The mischievous Zvereva always seemed to find a way of helping her sometimes nervous partner to relax. They won four of the five Wimbledon finals they contested in the 1990s and gave enormous pleasure to their legion of fans around the world.

BILLIE JEAN MOFFITT KING/ROSIE CASALS (1967, 1968, 1970, 1971 & 1973)
KING/KAREN SUSMAN (1962), MARIA BUENO (1965), BETTY STOVE (1972) & MARTINA NAVRATILOVA (1979).

Billie Jean King contributed a whole chapter to Wimbledon's doubles' history as well as singles. Billie Jean and her fellow American Rosie Casals, another fine volleyer, were virtually invincible between 1967 and 1973 when they claimed five titles. Billie Jean's total of 20 titles in singles, doubles and mixed at Wimbledon is a record she proudly now shares with Martina Navratilova. How appropriate, then, that it was the Czech-born left-hander who helped her to surpass Elizabeth Ryan's total of 19 with their doubles win in 1979. Altogether Billie Jean would win 10 ladies' doubles titles at Wimbledon with five different partners.

SERENA WILLIAMS/VENUS WILLIAMS (2000, 2002, 2008 & 2009)

When Venus Williams won her first Wimbledon singles title in 2000, she and sister Serena also went on to win the doubles. They were the first sisters to do so (and indeed the first unseeded pair, unseeded because they had played little tournament doubles). In 2002, they repeated their feat, this time after Serena had won the singles. It seemed that these two remarkable sisters would dominate the tennis world for the next decade with their raw power and extraordinary athleticism. That it did not quite happen was due partly to a series of niggling injuries and partly to a growing interest in

other pursuits. Nevertheless, after Venus had won an all-sister battle for her fifth singles title in 2008, a third doubles crown was also claimed and they followed that by recapturing the Olympic title they had first won together in Sydney eight years earlier. It was no surprise when they won Wimbledon again in 2009.

CARA BLACK/LIEZEL HUBER (2005 & 2007)
BLACK/RENNAE STUBBS (2004)

Cara Black grew up trying to emulate her two older brothers, Byron and Wayne, who both became highly ranked doubles players on the men's tour. The

experience was invaluable. Cara won her first Wimbledon title in 2004 with Australia's Rennae Stubbs. In 2005 she teamed with America's Liezel Huber, who was born in South Africa. Overnight they became one of the best pairs in the world with two wins at Wimbledon as well as an Australian crown and two prestigious year-end WTA Championship titles.

MIXED

We should not forget the mixed doubles, which so often provides a skilful and entertaining end to The Championships.

Among the ladies, three-time winners with various partners include Elizabeth Ryan, Suzanne Lenglen, Louise Brough, Darlene Hard and Martina Navratilova. As to the men, Fred Stolle also has three victories to his name with different partners.

Pride of place, though, goes to three pairs with at least three Wimbledon titles together. The first was the highly effective American pairing of Vic Seixas/Doris Hart who recorded successive titles together in 1953, 1954 and 1955 (and each also won with other partners). They were followed by the formidable Australian pairing of Ken Fletcher/Margaret Smith (later Mrs Court) who were dominant in the next decade and collected four titles together in 1963, 1965, 1966 and 1968. They were in turn matched by the great Australian/American pairing of Owen Davidson/ Billie Jean King whose four successes came in 1967, 1971, 1973 and 1974.

6	6	7	6
3	7	6	4

Boris Becker's arrival at Wimbledon in 1985 was unforgettable. Unseeded, the 17-year-old German thrilled the Centre Court on his way to the final. Would he become Wimbledon's youngest men's singles champion?

BECKER TAKES TITLE AND MAKES HISTORY

The Daily Telegraph
8th April 1985
By John Parsons

Wimbledon rose to acclaim a remarkable new champion yesterday as Boris Becker, still more than four months away from his 18th birthday, stormed to a 6-3 6-7 7-6 6-4 defeat of Kevin Curren.

In a three hour 18 minutes contest which began almost tamely but then developed into a gripping feast, Becker became not only the youngest winner in the 109 years of the Championships and the first German to triumph, but above all, the first to do so unseeded.

Despite the prediction by Johan Kriek after Becker had beaten him in the Queen's Club final that this amazing youngster would win Wimbledon, it was still almost impossible to believe it had happened.

Curren was broken the first time he served, which was enough to cost him the opening set. He never went even remotely close to recapturing the explosive serving form which had knocked out former champions John McEnroe and Jimmy Connors in previous rounds.

Curren never settled into his game while the fearless, uninhibited Becker suddenly lifted his in the most dynamic fashion after an escape which allowed him to take the third set. Striking the ball with almost frightening force, Becker first broke back, then delivered three thundering aces in the game which followed and from then on maintained an unfailing level of willpower and determination which ultimately proved decisive. Tumbling and diving, he kept going wholeheartedly for winners.

Becker, almost two years the junior of the previous youngest champion, Wilfred Baddeley, in 1891, was in no mood to offer Curren even a glimmer of a chance.

It was far from one of the greatest Wimbledon finals. But because of the excitement of watching such a charismatic new prodigy and the historical significance surrounding his success, it is one which will always be remembered.

UNBEATABLE!

It's the end of an era says Martina as her record bid is dashed

Nineteen-year-old Steffi Graf, already champion in Australia and France, found herself 5-7 0-2 down against the defending champion Martina Navratilova. Could Steffi recover and join Boris Becker as a German singles champion at Wimbledon?

Sunday Express

3rd July 1988

By Barry Newcombe

The fortress crumbled, then fell taking with it Martina Navratilova and all her dreams and leaving Steffi Graf the formidable new queen of Wimbledon.

The dynasty set up by Martina was over. The Czech left-hander first played at Wimbledon in 1973, the year that Steffi was given a cut down racket by her father, Peter, who led the arm-raising salute to her on the Centre Court.

Martina went on to haul in her eighth Wimbledon singles titles last year but the history-making ninth was denied her by the 19-year-old West German.

The bare facts of Steffi's first victory – 5-7 6-2 6-1 in 93 minutes – do not disclose that she took the final by storm. She captured 12 of the last 13 games in an emphatic statement of a change at the top of the women's game.

Steffi is set to dominate Wimbledon, and everywhere else, after this victory. She will build on this performance because she broke two barriers on the same day – one a great player, the other the game's greatest title.

Unlike Martina, who has always had to battle for supremacy against the rugged challenge of Chris Evert,

no one seems able to live with the pace and power of Steffi and her master stroke, her forehand. That forehand became the force of the final. Steffi thrived on it – and it broke Martina, just as it has broken so many lesser opponents.

The remarkable young German has won 21 consecutive Grand Slam matches this year for the loss of one set in yesterday's final and marches on to complete the Slam in the US Open in September. Not since Maureen Connolly in 1953 has one so young been in the reckoning.

"Yes," said Martina. "It's definitely the end of a chapter."

It was the third final in a row between the two leading men of the day. Boris Becker, the youngest ever champion five years previously and already with three titles to his name at Wimbledon, against the elegant Swede Stefan Edberg. Both were strong, attacking players. The 1990 final certainly lived up to its billing.

Edberg equal to epic

The Independent
9th July 1990
By John Roberts

The rumour that ground safety alterations had drained Wimbledon of atmosphere were proved to be unfounded on a bright and breezy afternoon, when those two young rivals, Stefan Edberg and Boris Becker, turned their third consecutive men's singles final into an epic.

What the match lacked in finesse was more than compensated for in excitement, and a capacity, all-seated Centre Court crowd roared its approval as the contest dramatically changed character before being settled by an unexpected twist of fortune in the fifth set.

Becker, the defending champion, was the player destined to fail this time after creating great theatre by hauling himself back into the match from two sets down, sets which had seen his famous serve mocked by the power, accuracy and consistency of Edberg's returns.

He then broke Edberg to take a 3-1 lead in the final set, at which stage it was difficult to imagine that the 24-year-old Swede would keep such a bold, confident competitor from a fourth Wimbledon title. It transpired that Becker was capable of handing the title back to his rival.

Serving, Becker double-faulted and

then made two astonishing errors with the forehand volley. The second one, steered wide of a vacant court on break point, proved to be the slender difference between winning and losing.

A few years ago, it would have been difficult to believe that Edberg could find

the resolve to escape from a corner as tight as this one, or that Becker would flinch with an opponent at his mercy. But if sporting events always went according to pre-conception nobody would camp outside the All England Club waiting in hope for one of those precious seats.

PLAY IS SUSPENDED

IN THE EVENT OF RAIN
SPECTATORS ARE REQUESTED
NOT TO RAISE UMBRELLAS
UNTIL PLAY HAS BEEN STOPPED

IT RAINS IN ENGLAND. In SW19, the eyes of the spectators on the Centre Court catch that familiar sight... the court coverers gathering at the back of the court, dark clouds moving in menacingly, the Referee ready to give the sign to the umpire. Play is suspended.

The team of court coverers moves quickly. Keeping the court dry has always been a challenge and a priority. It takes the team, trained during the two weeks prior to The Championships, less than half-a-minute to cover the court. The record is 22 seconds. A team of 17 is needed to cover the court. Two more remove the net and two remove the umpire and linespersons' chairs. Pushing the umpire's chair with the umpire still in it started in 2001.

The risk of interruptions or delays for rain or, worse, abandonment of the day's play, has been ever-present. The vagaries of the British weather mean that the tournament is almost always disrupted at some point by rain. Indeed, the first Championships at Church Road in 1922 were not completed until the Wednesday of the third week with the men's final being played on the Monday.

The British are a patient lot,

God wot

On the Centre Court they stand and stare

At the ghosts of players who are not there

And grin and bear

Their lot

They've queued all night, they've stood all day

So they have to stay -

To display their ardour, quite undismayed,

'Til the decision, so long delayed,

Gives rain again the final say -

Call it a day

(From *Wimbledon: Centre Court of the Game*, Max Robertson, BBC (1981))

2.30 ROLEX

THANK YOU FOR YOUR PATIENCE DURING THIS RAIN DELAY. FURTHER INFORMATION ON THE WEATHER WILL FOLLOW SHORTLY

⋏ The new information boards carry a familiar message | Maria Sharapova is only one step ahead of the court coverers ➤

The accompanying photographs tell their own stories of past Centre Court experiences in the rain. Most spectators, bearing a British resolve, made the best of it, waiting patiently. Little could be done… another announcement was made:

"LADIES AND GENTLEMEN, MAY I HAVE YOUR ATTENTION PLEASE. I AM AFRAID THE BRIEF SHOWER WHICH WE HAVE JUST HAD DOES NOT MEAN THAT THERE WILL NOT BE LONGER PERIODS OF RAIN ARRIVING SHORTLY…"

CHRIS GORRINGE, CHIEF EXECUTIVE, 2002

Announcements have in recent years been made for the Club by former BBC radio sports commentator Tony Adamson. He delivered the familiar message in his own style:

"THE RAIN APPEARS TO HAVE ABATED FOR THE MOMENT. THE PLAN IS TO DEFLATE THE COVERS, UNCOVER THE COURTS, AND IF PLAY IS DUE TO START IN THE NOT TOO DISTANT FUTURE, THEN I SHALL BE BACK TO YOU. THANK YOU."

"I SUGGEST A CUP OF TEA AND A BUN, AND THEN WE SHOULD BE ABLE TO RESUME PLAY AFTER THAT…"

Before the cover could be raised the lifting cable had to be attached

(centre) Former head groundsman, Bob Twynam, supervising the covering procedure

The canvas cover then became a tent before a patient but wet audience

One of the worst downpours occurred in 1985.
A spectacular thunderstorm hit Wimbledon shortly
before 2pm on the second Friday with one and a half inches of rain falling
in 20 minutes. One spectator, a Miss Anne Rundle, aged 23, even took the
opportunity to swim in one of the entrance passageways to the Centre
Court which was flooded to a depth of three feet. "*I'd got so wet anyhow, so I
thought to myself, 'What the hell?'*" she said. "*I'd do anything to get on to the
Centre Court.*"

Sometimes there has been impromptu entertainment. Cliff Richard,
attending as a member one very wet day in 1996, gave a rendition of
Summer Holiday and other songs with an accompaniment of stewards and
players and much to the pleasure and amusement of the public on Centre
Court that day. But even Cliff agrees that it was a 'one-off'. In 2001, there
was a memorable interview with former US President Bill Clinton.

Rain delays are frustrating for both players and fans. It is difficult for
players to produce their best form with constant breaks — sometimes even
stretching a match over two or more days. Struggling to receive serve in an
important match in evening gloom with grass dampening underfoot is
unsatisfactory. Most players are, though, more careful than one competitor
in 1907:

"*When persistent rain stopped play, Mrs Hillyard ate a 'fearful' tea: two Bath
buns, six or seven slices of bread and butter, three or four cups of tea, six or seven
biscuit cakes, two or three slices of other cake and three plates of strawberries. No
sooner had she finished than the Referee requested her to play. She lost her semi-final
match and complained bitterly to the Committee.*"

For the millions of television viewers worldwide, coverage of a grey
Wimbledon with a green tent over Centre Court, or alternatively hours of
repeats, has limited appeal. In the 21st century this did little to promote
Wimbledon as one of the world's great sporting events.

Could the Centre Court be given a retractable roof for use when it
was wet?

6	6	6	1	6
7	4	4	6	4

Andre Agassi, after missing a number of years, now loved Wimbledon. The colourful American from Las Vegas was showing what could be done in the modern age by a talented baseliner who was not afraid to stand up against the power players. But did he have the nerve to win at the highest level?

Agassi wins first grand slam title

Flamboyant American completes rise from court jester to king at Wimbledon

The Times

6th July 1992

By Andrew Longmore

One of the briefest romances in the history of the Championships ended in the perfect marriage on the Centre Court yesterday. Amid scenes of high emotion, Andre Agassi out hit and outlasted Goran Ivanisevic 6-7 6-4 6-4 1-6 6-4 to become the unlikeliest Wimbledon champion of all.

In two hours and 50 minutes of quickfire brilliance, the street urchin with the flowing locks became king of the turf, the rebel found a cause and the bastion of tradition gained a champion coined in the mint of Las Vegas: earring, squirrel's tail hair, baggy shorts, bicycle pants and all.

And, what is more, he did it the hard way. Taking on the big servers with nothing but quickness of eye and feet to protect him and proving to all that, on the biggest stage of all, he had the heart to prevail.

It was a refreshing final, full of character, life and novelty, played at a rip-roaring pace between two of the game's young pretenders.

When the Croat netted a backhand volley on match point, Agassi fell flat on his face on the grass he had spurned for three years and wept unashamedly. All his dreams had come true, all his worst nightmares after three defeats in grand slam finals had been banished in the very place he had least expected fulfilment.

Where his fellow American, Pete Sampras, had drooped beneath the hail of aces from Ivanisevic in the semi-final, Agassi held firm, feeding off the scraps of second serves until offered the final ironic crumb of a double-fault.

Agassi's only regret was that he had missed three years of the tournament since 1988. "It's sad. This tournament has given my life so much and it's a shame I didn't respect it earlier. This is the greatest title in the world and this is my greatest achievement" the new champion said.

Graf tumbles to historic defeat

On paper it was just another routine first round match; the world no.1 Steffi Graf, champion for the past three years, with five singles titles in all to her illustrious name, against the American Lori McNeil, ranked a modest 22 and unseeded. Yet there was an ominous sense of foreboding in the air. The leaden skies and a swirling wind threatened stormy interruptions. In this Wagnerian atmosphere the champion looked anxious.

The Guardian

22nd June 1994

By David Irvine

Over the years Steffi Graf has given so much to the Wimbledon legend. Five times a winner since 1988 she has even threatened to overtake Martina Navratilova's record.

But yesterday, in the Centre Court gloom, she contributed another, bleaker chapter, becoming the first women's champion in the tournament's history to lose in the opening round. A packed and disbelieving crowd saw her lose 7-5 7-6 to the 30-year-old American Lori McNeil. It was one of the most astonishing upsets ever in the women's game.

What would normally be regarded as a formality became a painful and searching three-part examination of Graf's game – character, concentration and will. She failed. Incredibly she failed. She arrived at Wimbledon having won her last 21 matches there, only to fall at the first hurdle. She played as if she had still not got over the awful drubbing by Mary Pierce in Paris. Her approach was that of a nervous, fumbling discontent desperately trying to spark the fires that had made her, rightly, queen of the game.

Though a commoner by contrast, it has to be said that McNeil played with royal serenity and flourish. That her victory was deserved nobody would question. She played a brilliant, shrewd and controlled match and, although behind in the second set, produced a stunningly effective game at 4-5 to wrest back the initiative.

For all the torture Graf endured there was much from both players to admire as the contest built towards its climax. "But she was better than me, that was obvious" admitted Graf. "She served much better and I just didn't have a very good time. On the important points I never really played right".

McNeil is a genuine grass court expert. She hustled Graf at the net and when the German attempted to control the forecourt herself she was taunted with perfectly judged lobs. She said: "It feels great. It's definitely the best win of my career and I'm just happy I'm through to the next round."

4	6	7
6	1	5

Graf's hard-fought win proves her greatness

Since her first win at Wimbledon in 1988, the year she joined Maureen Connolly and Margaret Court as the only women to win the Grand Slam, Steffi Graf had become outstandingly the best of the women players. Yet in 1995 the five-time champion was under serious threat from a bubbling Spaniard whose sunny smile captivated the crowd. Arantxa Sanchez Vicario, at 17, the youngest French Open champion in 1989, was beginning to believe in herself on grass.

The Times
9th July 1995
By Richard Evans

After a year of pain and self doubt, Steffi Graf bestrode the Centre Court again as Queen of Wimbledon, beating back a furious and worthy challenge from Arantxa Sanchez Vicario to win her sixth title 4-6 6-1 7-5.

The match built to such a splendid climax that it will have done much to ease the problems facing women's tennis as it struggles to find other players capable of challenging the top four or five stars.

It all started so promisingly for Sanchez. Amazingly, this tiny player, all 5ft 6ins of her, dropped only four points on her serve in the entire first set. Rattled by her opponent's composure, Graf suddenly cracked in the seventh game missing three consecutive forehands to drop serve and then helping the Spaniard serve out for the set with two backhand errors.

The momentum changed in the fourth game of the second set when Sanchez punched a forehand volley long. The breach was made and a double fault helped Graf to another break, giving her the set 6-1.

In the final set many of the rallies were heart-stopping and the whole spectacle built to an epic climax in the 11th game when no fewer than 32 points were played, encompassing 13 deuces with Sanchez reaching game point seven times and Graf needing six break points before she managed the decisive breach. "No game ever meant so much to me at such a stage" said Graf. Graf kept pressing, reluctant

to get to the net unless there was a clear opportunity, but Sanchez kept enticing her to the forecourt, teasing her with deft angles and the occasional booming forehand.

But in the end you could hear the sound of the castanets fading into the sunset. This was Graf's day to reclaim her rightful throne. She broke and served out regally for the match and raced off court to embrace her parents.

TIM HENMAN d.
YEVGENY KAFELNIKOV

7	6	6	4	7
6	3	7	6	5

Playing in his third Wimbledon, the 21–year–old British No. 1 Tim Henman had been given a tough draw – a first round meeting against the new French Open champion Yevgeny Kafelnikov of Russia. Yet in his losing match against Pete Sampras the previous year Henman was already beginning to show the kind of form on grass that suggested a bright future

Henman rally earns stunning five set victory over Kafelnikov

The Daily Telegraph

26th June 1996

By John Parsons

Tim Henman's reputation as Britain's finest prospect for years was gloriously, courageously and spectacularly demonstrated in front of an ecstatic Centre Court crowd at Wimbledon last night as he dramatically beat fifth seed Yevgeny Kafelnikov, the French Open singles and doubles champion, in the first round.

In a few unbelievable minutes, at the end of a match lasting three hours 36 minutes, Henman went from saving two match points with aces when trailing 5-3 in the final set to being cheered off court as a 7-6 6-3 6-7 4-6 7-5 winner. Over those last nail biting points, it was as if almost everyone in the crowd was playing every point with a player who less than two years ago was hobbling around on crutches with his career threatened by a broken ankle.

It was the manner of Henman's performance – full of character as well as skill, after chances to have won in straight sets slipped away – as much as the result itself which was so impressive. It was easily the best British performance since John Lloyd beat fourth-seeded Roscoe Tanner in four sets in 1977.

"Until you've played in front of a crowd like that you can't understand," said Henman. "They were absolutely phenomenal – one of the reasons I was able to turn things around and pull it out".

Few held out much hope for Henman when, having been broken in the first game of the final set, he faced defeat at 3-5, 15-40. Yet once those two match points were so bravely saved, the rest was pure theatre. Fine returns – and another Kafelnikov double-fault – meant Henman broke back to 5-5, held for 6-5 and then broke the bewildered Russian again to begin the British celebrations.

PLAY RESUMES

TALK OF A SLIDING ROOF for Centre Court had been around for many years. Yet the technical challenges involved were always going to be great. A roof could not be a solid, sliding structure. That would be too bulky and dark when 'open'. How could you prevent condensation and protect the grass within a 'closed' bowl? How could you ensure light still adequately reached the growing grass? How would you fit a modern high-tech ventilation system into an 80-year old building?

A roof for Centre Court would not solve all problems caused by rain during the tournament – but it would be a major step. It would ensure tennis action for 15,000 paying spectators. The tournament would benefit from certainty of play at important moments, particularly in the final stages. Millions of television viewers worldwide would be guaranteed live tennis to watch whatever the weather. As Tim Phillips, Chairman of the All England Club, said: "*We owe it to tennis fans to investigate all the possibilities for play to take place even if it is raining.*"

Going into the 21st century, advances in technology started to make a roof a possibility. It would, though, need an innovative design and structure to meet the particular requirements of Centre Court. Specialist sports stadia architects, HOK Sport, were commissioned and worked alongside consultant engineers. Satisfied that the design and technical issues could be resolved and the grass safeguarded, the decision that the project would go ahead was announced by the Club in January 2004.

> "CENTRE COURT IS THE JEWEL IN OUR CROWN AND WE ARE TRYING TO MAKE IT EVEN MORE PRECIOUS THAN IT ALREADY IS. WE WANT TO ENSURE THAT WIMBLEDON REMAINS THE TOURNAMENT THE PLAYERS WANT TO WIN AND THAT, INTERNATIONALLY, EVERYONE WANTS TO WATCH"
>
> TIM PHILLIPS. CLUB CHAIRMAN, JANUARY 2004

Construction commenced under main contractors, Galliford Try. The roof was actually assembled in part and tested off-site in Rotherham, Yorkshire before components were transported to SW19 and re-assembled. And, of course, each summer the site was cleared ready for The Championships.

For the 2009 Championships the Centre Court proudly displayed its new retractable roof.

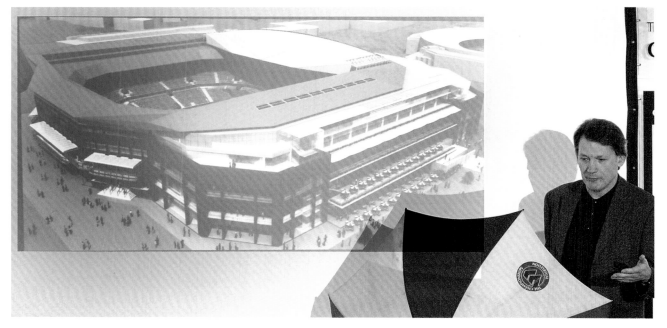

◄ Rod Sheard, a direction of HOK Sport, presents the project to the press in January 2004

A computer generated impression of the roof 'closed' ➤

The Centre Court "wrapped for Christmas" in November 2006

An initial truss is lifted into position, April 2008

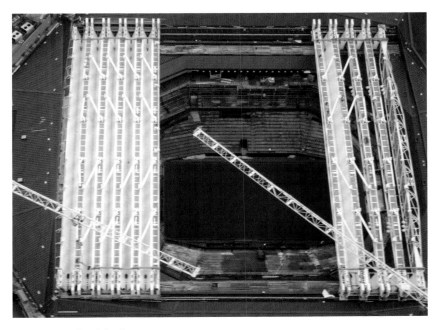

An aeriel view as the roof takes shape

"THE MOST EXCITING MOMENT
OF THE CENTRE COURT
REFURBISHMENT PROJECT HAS BEEN
THE 1,000 TONNE CRANE DOING
THE BIG LIFT OF THE FIXED TRUSS.
WE DID ONE YEAR'S PREPARATION
AND THEN THE TRUSS WAS LIFTED
AND ASSEMBLED IN A WEEK. WE
WERE DELIGHTED IT FITTED!"
TOM McNULTY, SENIOR ENGINEER,
GALLIFORD TRY

Fabric is installed within the trusses, October 2008

HOW THE ROOF WORKS

The retractable roof over the Centre Court is a 'folding fabric concertina'. This allows it to be folded into a compressed area when not in use over the court, as well as being translucent enough to provide an 'open' feel when the roof is closed. Approximately 5,200 square metres of a special waterproof and flexible fabric have been used.

The retractable roof is divided into two sections with a total of nine bays of fabric – four bays in one section and five in the other. Each bay is clamped on either side by prismatic steel trusses. There are ten trusses spanning approximately 75 metres across the court. The ends of each truss are supported by a set of wheels that move along a track positioned on the new fixed perimeter roof of the Centre Court.

Both sections of the roof are normally parked to the north in the months outside of The Championships. This allows maximum sunlight onto the court. During The Championships and in preparation for closing the roof, one section (with five bays) is parked in its folded state at the north end of the court while the other (with four bays) is parked at the south end.

The retractable roof is operated by a computer controlled system. The control console is located in a secure room within the Centre Court building with a communication link to the Referee.

The trusses move under electro-mechanical power, each truss having a set of

motorised bogeys at each end operating in tandem. Once in the extended position, the trusses are locked and braced. As the trusses move apart, the fabric (always under tension) is pulled upwards to create the full canopy over the court until the two sections meet in an overlapping seam above the middle of the court. The arch shape

‹ Fabric installation is nearly complete, January 2009

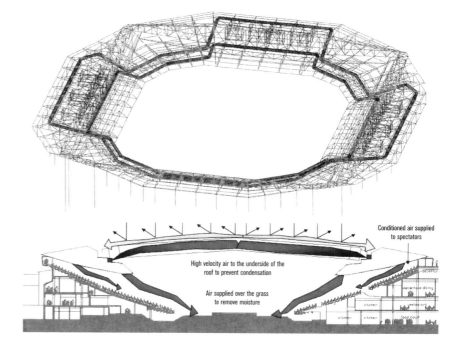

Conditioned air supplied to spectators

High velocity air to the underside of the roof to prevent condensation

Air supplied over the grass to remove moisture

to the tops of the trusses helps the structure to shift, if necessary, significant volumes of rainwater that could fall on it when the roof is closed. (A drainage system ensures that rainwater is channelled below the Centre Court before being pumped out to the lake in nearby Wimbledon Park.) The arch-shaped roof is also designed to combat snow and high winds. The height from the court to the bottom of the trusses has been set to provide sufficient clearance for high lobs during a match – 16 metres.

⌅ Diagrams, courtesy of M-E Engineers, showing the primary ductwork in the fixed perimeter roof (top) and the air-flow system to prevent condensation

A vital feature is the air-flow system. The new fixed perimeter roof incorporates air-handling units fed from chiller machines on the west side of the grounds. The system is designed to ensure that the Centre Court bowl, when the retractable roof is closed, provides an internal environment conducive to tennis. When closed, the temperature is maintained at 24°C (plus/minus two degrees) with approximately 50 per cent humidity. Air is circulated within the bowl in order to prevent condensation on either the roof or the grass. Supplementary sports lighting is provided, primarily through uplighters, at a level sufficient to support play into the evening.

Work on the roof in November 2008, showing one of the tracks on which the trusses move when closing

HOW IT IS USED

The retractable roof, when closed, provides a first class, consistent and safe (non-slippery) playing environment. Made of material that allows natural light to reach the grass even when closed, the roof offers protection to the grass surface under all adverse weather conditions. Importantly, the improved contours and slightly larger aperture of the new fixed roof also enables more sunlight to reach the court's surface when the sliding roof is open during the other months of the year. This improves growing conditions for the grass, particularly at the more shady southern end.

The roof is closed primarily to protect play from inclement weather during The Championships. Play is suspended while the roof closes, before being resumed once both the court surface and the bowl of the stadium have attained the optimum conditions for playing tennis.

The roof closes in approximately 10 minutes. When the roof is being closed for rain, the court cover continues to be used immediately play is suspended in order to protect the grass in the usual way while closure is in progress. After the roof has been closed, play resumes within a period of approximately 20 to 30 minutes, depending on ambient weather.

It is not intended to schedule night sessions of play but the roof now gives flexibility to ensure that matches can be completed in the event of bad light.

The decision to close (or open) the roof is taken by the Referee. The general practice is that, once the roof has been closed for a match, it stays closed until the finish of that particular match.

The retractable roof nears completion in late January 2009

SOME CENTRE COURT ROOF NUMBERS

75 – metres, the span of the moving roof trusses (width of a football pitch = 68m)

3,000 – tonnes, combined weight (both fixed and moving) of the roof

6,000 – square metres, area of retractable roof when fully deployed

7,500 – Wimbledon umbrellas, needed to cover the same area as the retractable roof

143,000 – amount in litres of conditioned air that the air flow system supplies to the bowl per second

290 million – tennis balls you could fit in the Centre Court with the roof closed

---

"IT IS IMPORTANT TO STRESS THAT WE STILL SEE WIMBLEDON AS FUNDAMENTALLY AN OUTDOOR SUMMER'S TOURNAMENT. WE ARE USING THE ROOF AS AN INSURANCE POLICY. WE ARE CONSTANTLY TRYING TO IMPROVE AND WE THINK THE ROOF WILL BE A GREAT ADVANTAGE"

IAN RITCHIE. CLUB CHIEF EXECUTIVE, JANUARY 2009

Katherine Jenkins entertains the crowd as part of *A Centre Court Celebration*, when the new roof was closed in public for the first time

A CENTRE COURT CELEBRATION

The new roof was nearly ready for action. First, though, the All England Club
wanted to test the new roof and the air management system with live tennis in front
of a capacity crowd. On Sunday, 17th May 2009 a memorable and unique event was
held: *A Centre Court Celebration* was both a test and a reminder that tennis is still a
sport to be enjoyed for its own sake.

While the roof was closing, musical entertainment was provided for the 15,000
spectators by singers Katherine Jenkins, Faryl Smith and Blake – and spontaneous
applause broke out when the two halves of the roof finally came together.

There followed three exhibition matches. First the husband-and-wife team of
Andre Agassi and Steffi Graf, both legendary Wimbledon champions, played a set of
mixed doubles against the ever-popular Tim Henman and Kim Clijsters. It was the
invitation to take part in this special event that persuaded the Belgian to return to
the women's tour after two years of retirement, a
decision fully justified when she won the 2009

◄ Faryl Smith and Katherine Jenkins in the
Club's main entrance hall

US Open later in the year. The two men then played a pro-set and finally there was another pro-set between the two ladies, both played in a marvellous spirit.

Fortunately, for once, it started to rain during play so the occasion became a true test. Happily, the new roof, the lighting, the air management system and the playing conditions all came through with flying colours. The Centre Court roof was ready for action during The Championships.

2009 CHAMPIONSHIPS

Almost predictably, the 2009 Championships were one of the sunniest and hottest for many years. At times one suspected that the Centre Court crowd were even hoping for rain in order to see play under the roof for the first time in The Championships.

The occasion – and it was the only occasion throughout the fortnight – came on the second Monday when a rain shower interrupted the second set of the fourth round ladies' match between the top-seeded Russian, Dinara Safina, and Amelie Mauresmo of France, the 17th seed. The Referee made the decision to close the roof. Smoothly it closed and play resumed. Safina won the first point on Mauresmo's delivery and eventually won a close three-set match.

With further rain forecast, the roof remained closed. The first full match followed. It was another fourth round encounter between Britain's Andy Murray, seeded 3, and the Swiss no. 17 seed, Stanislas Wawrinka. The match became a titanic and pulsating drama with Murray recovering from an uncertain start and finally clinching a narrow victory at 6-3 in the final set. It was 10.38 pm.

As the evening moved towards Wimbledon's latest-ever finish, the All England Club was in darkness save for the extraordinary sight of the Centre Court shining brightly in the evening sky. From afar it looked like some extra-terrestrial spaceship. On a packed Aorangi terrace, the large screen was glowing in front of an expectant crowd. Enthralled and enthusiastic, they were cheering wildly as Murray inched his way towards victory. With an estimated 11.5 million viewers, the BBC cleared its prime time evening schedule to cover the historic match to the end – even delaying the main evening news by three-quarters of an hour.

Tennis under the roof was now a successful and stunning reality.

Amelie Mauresmo (foreground) – the first to hit a ball under the new roof in a Championship match – in her contest against Dinara Safina ➤

Andy Murray's five-set win over Stanislas Wawrinka under the roof ended at 10.38pm and the Aorangi picnic terrace was still packed (right)

6	7	6	6
7	6	4	2

Sampras lords it over Centre Court domain

Pete Sampras was seeking a record seventh Wimbledon singles title. He was up against Australia's finest, Pat Rafter, who had defeated Andre Agassi in a five set semi-final. It was a rain disrupted final and dusk was setting in. Sampras appeared to be carrying an injury. Could he claim that record?

The Daily Telegraph
10th July 2000
By Paul Hayward

The unthinkable happened on Centre Court. Pete Sampras looked vulnerable in a Wimbledon men's final. Rafter, the "typical Aussie bloke" as his coach, Tony Roche, once described him, was 4-1 up in the second set tiebreak after taking the first 7-6. But then a double-fault and a poor stroke let the six times Wimbledon champion back into a rain-interrupted match. Tension was mounting.

The only word which adequately describes Pete Sampras's hold on Centre Court over the last eight years is tyrannical. He is now officially the greatest player to have grabbed hold of a racket. "This is the best court in the world," Sampras said, through tears that fell in place of the spiteful rain.

Proprietorial, vigilant, spikely defiant, Sampras is all these things when his domination over the most sacred turf in tennis is challenged. Even performing moderately, as he did for long phases through the fading evening light, he conveys the impression that he can shift into a higher dimension at any moment. His adversaries have to get past the aura before they start chipping away at the man.

Rafter was still in a primary position with his one-set lead but was about to disappear in history's march. Sampras seized the next three sets in near darkness and was then overcome by the

magnitude of what he had achieved.

A short while back, he was asked why he shows so little of himself on court. Last night, at 8.57 p.m., he was euphoric and overcome, hugging his parents and mopping away the tears.

Hanging by a thin thread? For a while, yes, but it was only the golden twine of history.

Irrepressible Ivanisevic realises wildest dream

The Daily Telegraph
10th July 2001
By John Parsons

A final postponed to the third Monday saw the popular Croatian left-hander, Goran Ivanisevic, a three-time runner-up but now unseeded, up against the Australian favourite, Pat Rafter, losing finalist the previous year to Pete Sampras. The impassioned and good-natured support of a young Centre Court crowd of Croatians and Australians contributed to a supercharged atmosphere. The 2001 final was extraordinary.

Nine years after he squandered a wonderful opportunity to win the title Goran Ivanisevic at last achieved his lifelong dream of becoming Wimbledon champion - at the fourth attempt.

The wait proved to be as worthwhile and rewarding for him as it was for the 14,500 crowd who created and sustained the most incredible atmosphere throughout a three hour one minute match, which delivered all that was hoped for and much, much more in terms of emotion, courage, brilliant tennis and a nail biting finale.

Record books will show that Ivanisevic beat Pat Rafter in the first men's singles final postponed until the third Monday by the weather since 1922, 6-3 3-6 6-3 2-6 9-7. The scoreline, though, while hinting at the twists and turns, does not begin to convey the tension and drama which unfolded.

In years to come, anyone lucky enough to have been on Centre Court yesterday will be proud to relate how that they had been there at arguably the greatest final day in the 124-year history of The Championships. Certainly, it was the most thrilling I can recall in 42 years of reporting The Championships.

No wild-carded player had ever won a Grand Slam. This was a final matching not one but two crowd favourites. There has been no finer sportsman in tennis for the past decade than the pin-up Australian. There was glorious bedlam at every changeover. The suspense in the crowd was unbearable.

Another winning serve by Ivanisevic created a second match point. Again an overexcited Croatian double-faulted. A fantastic Rafter lob saved match point no.3 but on the fourth, the Australian yielded. This had been the final which had everything.

It was a moment to savour, a young pretender from Siberia challenging the two-time defending champion from the United States. Seventeen-year-old Maria Sharapova was facing the mighty Serena Williams who was expected to blow her off the court. It became a match to savour, full of drama and emotion.

Weeping beauty steals our hearts

Mail on Sunday

4th July 2004

By Malcolm Folley

From Russia to the Centre Court she came, radiating coquettish charm and a merciless tennis game.

And how we fell in love with the 17-year-old Maria Sharapova on an afternoon when summer returned to Wimbledon and women's tennis unveiled a new star rising from the unlikeliest place on earth.

From the frozen wastelands of Siberia, Sharapova journeyed to the summit of the game at the expense of a tennis dynasty who had treated Wimbledon's silverware as a family bauble these past four years.

Sharapova played with fortitude and without nerves, remarkable for a girl making only her fourth appearance on the most daunting tennis stage. The Centre Court is a cathedral but also a cauldron that can shred the ambition of all but the strongest.

After 22 minutes Sharapova led 5-1. She was returning serve with brilliant anticipation and her backhand was formidable. Williams was in a Siberian storm with little hope of shelter. The first set belonged to Sharapova in a mere 30 minutes.

Her hours, days, weeks, months and years spent working on the practice courts of Florida and California, after her father had convinced Nick Bollittieri to enrol his daughter in his fabled tennis academy, had been dedicated to arriving at this point. Her two years spent apart from her mother as a seven-year-old seemed but the blink of an eye right here, right now.

Sharapova broke Williams' serve – and heart – in the ninth game of the second set before stepping to the line to act out the fantasy of a thousand practices. She really was serving for the Championship and, when it was hers, she threw her racket and sank to her knees in tears. From Russia, she had a story to tell through the ages.

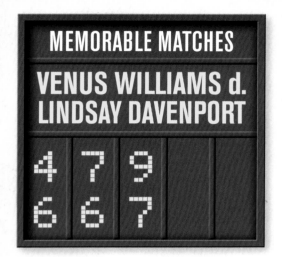

4	7	9	
6	6	7	

Marathon woman Venus ascendant again

The Independent
4th July 2005
By Ronald Atkin

The 2005 final exemplified the ultimate power in women's tennis. America's Venus Williams, champion in 2000 and 2001 and back on the final stage, against her compatriot Lindsay Davenport, champion in 1999. The outcome was uncertain until the final point.

In the end, the battle went to the braver, fitter woman, the one who struck out successfully every time disaster threatened to engulf her.

So Venus Williams was entitled to her cavorting leap of delight as she claimed her third Wimbledon title in six years on an afternoon of high drama and record breaking by defeating Lindsay Davenport 4-6 7-6 9-7. The match shattered the tournament's longevity record for this occasion. At two hours 45 minutes, it eclipsed the previous record of two hours, 28 minutes set in 1970 by the Margaret Court/Billie Jean King final.

Davenport missed a match point at 5-4 in a third set which lasted 78 minutes while struggling with the onset of back trouble. She could have won, and would have but for some courageous counter-attacking by Williams whenever her back was pressed to the wall. Beforehand, Davenport was talking about the "close, crazy matches" they had played. This, the 27th, out-crazied the lot.

In the second set, riveting by virtue of its wild swings, Davenport broke for a 6-5 lead. Serving for the match, she was broken without managing to rescue a single point. Williams levelled the match by winning the tiebreak seven points to four with an emphatic forehand.

At 6-7 in the final set Williams wobbled yet again, two points from oblivion, but she fought back noisily and brilliantly to stay alive. At 7-7 it was Davenport's turn to be pitched into trouble and she failed to escape, broken by a stunning Williams forehand.

Williams served for the Championship. As a final Davenport forehand rattled into the net Williams leapt high into the air and after accepting the appropriately named Venus Rosewater Dish from the Duke of Kent and the prizewinner's cheque for £600,000, she indulged in more leaps of sheer joy. Who can blame her after the pain and misery she has endured in coming back from long spells of injury and poor form to capture the greatest prize in the women's game as the 14th seed? Cavorting was in order.

QUIET PLEASE!

THE FANS are vital to the atmosphere of Centre Court. Spectators come from many different walks of life – and many different countries. They share an enthusiasm for tennis and the special occasion of a match on Centre Court, whether a first round battle or a final. It has always been so. (*Overleaf, enthusiastic fans queue to watch Fred Perry's first final in 1934.*)

GETTING A TICKET

A ticket for the Centre Court is one of the most prized in the world of sport. Demand for Wimbledon tickets has exceeded supply for most of the history of The Championships. Equitable distribution of tickets is inevitably a subject which causes much debate.

The Club's policy has always been to protect the number of tickets allocated to the general public because it is the Club's firm belief that these genuine tennis and Wimbledon fans should have access to their favourite event and that they contribute greatly to the special atmosphere of The Championships. Despite the demand which would justify higher prices, the policy of the Club has been to maintain the prices of tickets at a level which remains affordable to a wide range of the public and to establish means of ticket distribution which ensure access to a large number of genuine tennis fans.

Only the holders of Debentures (who have helped to finance the major capital projects at the ground), members of the Club and council members of the LTA are entitled to obtain tickets as a matter of right. A small number of tickets (less than 10 per cent) are available for corporate hospitality and overseas package tours through the Club and its official licensed agents.

The Club takes great care to ensure, so far as it can, that tickets go to the people and sectors contemplated by this carefully structured ticket distribution system. All tickets (other than Debenture holder tickets) are strictly non-transferable and may not be sold including over the internet. Action is taken against touts. Any person seeking to gain entry with a ticket acquired in breach of these conditions will not have a valid ticket and may be refused entry.

⬈ A seat for the Centre Court on finals day is one of the hottest tickets in world sport

◀ Roger Federer on his lap of honour following his fifth win in 2007

THE ANNUAL BALLOT

The majority of Centre Court tickets are sold in advance via the Club's annual public ballot and the LTA's schemes for tennis clubs and supporters of British tennis.

A public ballot was first introduced in 1924 owing to the huge demand for tickets. Wimbledon's public ballot is unique among the tennis Grand Slams. A combined public ballot for Centre Court, No. 1 Court and No. 2 Court seat tickets is held annually. There is a separate ballot for spaces allocated to wheelchair users and their escorts.

Only one application per household is permitted. The day and court for successful applicants are chosen randomly by a computerised selection process. The Wimbledon public ballot has itself become a national institution.

ON-DAY SALES

Wimbledon is also one of the very few major UK sporting events for which one can still buy premium tickets on the day. Around 500 Centre Court tickets (and a similar number for Courts 1 and 2) are reserved for on-day sale at the ground for the first nine days. The availability of these tickets is part of the reason for the unique on-day queues which are a feature of the Wimbledon scene and atmosphere.

Since 2007, tickets for around 500 Centre Court seats in the new terracing in the top rows of the court have been sold to the public via the internet through Ticketmaster every evening for the following day's play at the usual daily ticket price, plus a service charge.

Spectators leaving before the end of play are invited to offer their tickets for scanning or leave them in the red HSBC ticket resale bins, enabling tickets promptly to be resold at a nominal sum. Proceeds from the resale operation go to charity – currently doubled under arrangements with banking sponsor HSBC. The resale office within the

The overnight queues are a regular feature of Wimbledon

⋏ The red boxes allow departing fans to leave their tickets to be re-sold for charity. In 2009 more than £245,000 was raised for good causes

⋏ The large TV screen on Aorangi terrace is always popular with the fans, especially those with ground passes

Well-dressed fans in the 1920s, including those in the densely packed standing area behind the courtside seats ➤

grounds enables many to gain treasured access to the Centre Court later in the day.

For many, an enjoyable alternative is to acquire a ground entry ticket and to view the exciting action on the Centre Court shown on the large television screen seen from the Aorangi terrace.

"UNTIL YOU'VE PLAYED IN FRONT OF A CROWD LIKE THAT YOU CAN'T UNDERSTAND. THEY WERE ABSOLUTELY PHENOMENAL"
TIM HENMAN AFTER BEATING YEVGENY KAFELNIKOV IN 1996

Henmania was a feature at Wimbledon for more than a decade

ENTHUSIASM BUT RESPECT

Centre Court spectators are renowned for being amongst the most knowledgeable and appreciative fans in the tennis world. High enthusiasm but respect for the players is the order of the day.

Particular players will, of course, always be favourites and receive special support. The combination of seeing old favourites and new, exciting players is part of the Centre Court magic.

Fans may have changed in style of dress but not, it is clear, in their enjoyment and passion for tennis in this unique sporting venue – the jewel in Wimbledon's crown.

≺ Andy Murray thanks his supporters following his spectacular come-from-behind victory over Frenchman Richard Gasquet in 2008

≺ The young fans eagerly await an autograph from Andy Murray

"IT'S AN AWESOME FEELING TO HAVE THAT SORT OF SUPPORT"

ANDY MURRAY AFTER BEATING RICHARD GASQUET
IN 2008

MEMORABLE MATCHES

ROGER FEDERER d. RAFAEL NADAL

7	4	7	2	6
6	6	6	6	2

Roger Federer, the gloriously-talented Swiss superstar, had already won four successive championships. Bjorn Borg was in the Royal Box watching to see if his five-time record would be equalled. Federer's challenger was the world's no. 2, Rafael Nadal of Spain, ever more comfortable on grass. They were two rivals at the height of their games and of their mutual respect.

Federer gets Borg seal of approval by equalling famous five

Gallant Nadal takes champion to the limit

The Times

9th July 2007

By Neil Harman

Beneath Centre Court they hugged, the ice-cool icon of the 1970s and the similarly high class champion who has lifted the sport to a new, exalted plane three decades later. Roger Federer's fifth successive triumph at the high altar of tennis matched Björn Borg's record, set in 1980, and it was right that they should share a moment together, the two living embodiments of Wimbledon rule.

With his 7-6 4-6 7-6 2-6 6-2 victory over Rafael Nadal, the gallant Spaniard, Federer collected his eleventh grand slam tournament title from his record ninth consecutive final. Whichever way it turned out, something had to give for Borg – either Federer replicated his grass court sequence in SW19, or Nadal became the first person to win the French Open and Wimbledon within a month as was the Swede's norm when he ruled the sport with glacial beauty.

It took three hours and 46 minutes of classic cut-and-thrust tennis, of stroke-making and emotion that roused a full house on Centre Court, before Federer prevailed. It has been a long time since a British audience bore witness to a men's final of such potency, stoking a rivalry that has the basis of mutual respect.

It was a match of constant brilliance, mesmeric and unexpected shifts of emphasis, stunning bravado, and, ultimately, of that little edge on grass that Federer brings to the party as opposed to the subservience he feels to Nadal on clay.

It was the best men's final for a quarter of a century.

Nadal did all he could, recovering twice from a set down and, in the fifth set, standing twice within two points of pilfering Federer's serve.

What made the difference, he was asked? "Some points," Nadal replied. "He served better than me and on this surface the serve is more important. I played against the best of history and had good chances to win. I cannot say anything bad about my tournament or my game. Just congratulate him."

RAFAEL NADAL d. ROGER FEDERER

6	6	6	6	9
4	4	7	7	7

It was the dream final. The five-time champion facing, for the third year in a row, the Spanish left-hander who, a year earlier, had pushed him to the very limits. If Roger Federer was going to win a record sixth consecutive title, he would have to beat Rafael Nadal for the first time this year after suffering three defeats. This was indeed a battle of giants, a battle of wills, a battle for supremacy between the two greatest players of the present generation.

Battle of wills takes game to new level

The Daily Telegraph
7th July 2008
By Brough Scott

It ended in darkness but the pair of them had given us a blazing, eternal light. No sport, no playwright, has conjured up such magical theatre as those last three games as Rafa finally found his moment and threw himself triumphantly back on to the dew covered Wimbledon turf.

There had been moments in the first three sets when King Roger's head dipped in frustration at the prospect that his reign might be over without truly engaging in a fight. He was engaged now. Leading 7-6 in the fifth set with Rafa serving, he took the first point. Roger was just three points away from that so

coveted sixth title. Just three points, but they are hard to come by in the gathering gloom, with the crowd hushing down and Rafa Nadal going through to hold serve at the other end.

With the scores level, the drama moves forward almost too quickly. Roger is suddenly 15-40 down and once again facing into the unthinkable abyss he has been so close to before. Any earlier doubts of the full ferocious pride of this champion were dispelled as he crashed through a 125mph ace. But he could not hold the white bandana figure across the net. He was broken.

At ten past nine with well over 4½ hours of the unimaginably tense one-on-one combat Nadal was serving for the match in the gloaming. The stadium was so hushed that the only sound was the bouncing of the just-visible yellow ball. An owl was needed but Federer

must have night vision. Rafa now had two match points and his first serve was a bullet to Federer's backhand. In a flash of mesmerising, instinctive, reactive genius, it was slashed back past Rafa for a clear winner. It could not have happened, but it had.

Yet the end had to come – and with the force that is Nadal, come it would. For every magical Federer moment there was a Nadal return or, best of all, that inimitable whipped forehand

down the line winner. Now was the time, and the executioner's blow was self-inflicted, a Federer forehand dumped into the net. He and his opponent had given us something we will never forget.

As Rafa did his victory tour the camera flashes sparkled gold on the trophy. Of this night, of this most dramatic, most wondrous of tennis matches, the memories will always be golden too.

PREVIOUS SETS
SETS GAMES POINTS
7666 Andy RODDICK 214
6 5 v
5773 Roger FEDERER 215/9
CHALLENGES REMAINING
RODDICK
FEDERER

MEMORABLE MATCHES

ROGER FEDERER d. ANDY RODDICK

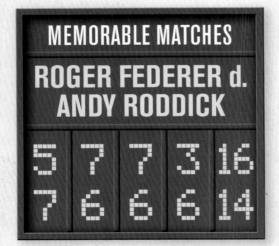

| 5 | 7 | 7 | 3 | 16 |
| 7 | 6 | 6 | 6 | 14 |

Eager to regain his crown, five-time champion Roger Federer faced the powerful American Andy Roddick in the 2009 final. They had competed for the title twice before. Would it be third time lucky for Roddick?

The Daily Telegraph
6th July 2009
By Ian Chadband

Swiss warrior forced to find new reserves

Just an hour after Federer had slapped the exclamation mark at the end of his title 'greatest of all time' after earning his record 15th grand slam in Wimbledon's seemingly endless final, he was already thinking ahead to putting his record number of grand slams beyond view.

Why not? After perhaps his most convincing performance yet of grace under pressure, a 27 year-old's will and talent from the gods could still take him anywhere he wants, presuming fatherhood does not derail him. Never before has he had to delve so feverishly into his endless reserves of champion's resolve to win a grand slam title. Never before has he looked more like a warrior than a wizard. To break the seemingly unbreakable, Federer offered a four and a quarter hour snapshot of his peerless career; the

brilliance, the glory but, most of all, the guts. He had to. Rod Laver, Bjorn Borg and Pete Sampras had come to pay homage to their successor. And, as they chatted to him afterwards, did the icons perhaps even recognise their superior?

In what has to be considered the equal of last year's unreal contest between Rafael Nadal and Federer – if not quite in quality, then at least in terms of the longevity of drama in that incredible last set – it was a tribute to Roddick's effort that the Swiss really did look as if he was forced to labour harder than ever before. This was a test of nerve. Not full of monumental rallies like last

year but, as Federer put it, more a throwback to the big serve and volley fests of yore. That last set could have come from a Hollywood western. Who would be the last man standing?

It may have been the American's best ever performance. Think of it; 10 times you have to serve to stay in the match against the greatest player of all time, and 10 times you do not blink. But when he lost at the 11th attempt it was not just because his body, wearied from a fortnight of rare battles, at last betrayed him. It was because Federer was too tough for the streetfighter.

At the key moment of the match Federer, trailing 2-6 in the second set tie-break, was facing four set points to go two sets down. Here was Federer in crisis, growing not shrinking. For how long will that tie-break torment Roddick? For ever and a day, probably.

But even then, he could not bring himself to hate his conqueror. No one can, because you can only celebrate a champion who is as humble and gracious off court as he is murderous on it. We are talking about a sportsman, and a sporting achievement, for the ages.

Published by Vision Sports Publishing Ltd 2010
© The All England Lawn Tennis & Croquet Club
ISBN 13: 978-1905326-82-2

The All England Lawn Tennis & Croquet Club
Church Road, Wimbledon,
London, SW19 5AE
www.wimbledon.org

Vision Sports Publishing Ltd
19-23 High Street, Kingston upon Thames,
Surrey, KT1 1LL
www.visionsp.co.uk

Edited by: John Barrett and Ian Hewitt
Editorial consultant: Jim Drewett
Photographic editor: Bob Martin
Design: Neal Cobourne, rkidesign@btinternet.com

Printed in China by Toppan Printing Co Ltd

VSP

PICTURE CREDITS

Front cover: The All England Lawn Tennis & Croquet Club – Neil Tingle

Back cover: The All England Lawn Tennis & Croquet Club

Inside pictures

The All England Lawn Tennis & Croquet Club/Wimbledon Lawn Tennis Museum:
5, 8, 10, 12, 16, 26, 28, 29, 30, 31, 32, 33, 34, 35, 36, 38, 39, 42, 47, 48, 50, 51, 52, 53, 54. 55,
56, 57, 58, 62, 63, 64, 65, 67, 69, 70, 71, 74, 75, 76, 77, 80, 82, 83, 86, 89, 90, 94, 95, 96, 97, 99,
100, 101, 105, 112, 114, 115, 117, 118, 120, 121, 122, 123, 124, 126, 132, 133, 141, 142, 143,
144, 147, 148, 153, 166, 170, 174, 186, 187, 189, 190, 191, 192, 193, 194, 201, 203, 207, 208,
209, 210, 211, 212, 214, 225, 226, 239, 240, 241, 244, 245, 246, 248, 249, 251;
Bob Martin – 6, 7, 11, 18, 19, 25, 59, 93, 121, 125, 130-31, 135, 146, 161, 162, 164, 165, 167,
237, 238, 242-243, 252, 254, 255; Tom Lovelock – 2, 24, 91, 96, 102, 103, 104, 107, 108, 111,
125, 128, 129, 130, 138, 139, 140, 172-181, 188, 217, 232, 243; Neil Tingle – 13, 21, 44, 45,
60, 116, 120, 215, 222, 223, 231, 233, 234; Tommy Hindley – 42, 253; Dominic Lipinski –
26, 96; Chris Raphael –136, 137, 232, 235; Glyn Campbell – 14; Chris Fowles – 227; Matt
Harris – 123; Glyn Kirk – 216; Tom McNulty – 227;
Peter Robertson – 41; Mike Valantes – 105

Michael Cole: 37, 41, 72, 73, 79, 81, 107, 110, 113, 126, 127, 143, 145, 149, 150, 157, 159,
160, 168, 169, 171, 182, 183, 184, 185, 194, 195, 196, 197, 198, 199, 200, 202, 204, 205, 206,
207, 218, 220, 221, 236, 237

Getty Images: Hulton Archive – 46, 66, 78, 87, 88, 106, 113; Clive Brunksill – 15, 123,
191, 217, 244; John Kelly – 119, 155; Bob Martin – 43, 158, 219; Popperfoto – 68, 236;
Simon Bruty – 40; Phil Cole – 163; Chris Cole – 156; Mike Hewitt – 17;
Steve Powell – 154; Ian Walton – 224

Sports Illustrated/Getty Images: 151, 152

Bongarts/Getty Images: 220

Julian Tatum: 61, 227, 228, 229, 230

Press Association: Rebecca Naden: 246

Reuters: Kevin Lamarque: 213; Ian Hodgson: 247

The Times: John Cassidy: 125

Shinji Oyama: 250

Every effort has been made to contact the copyright holders of the photographs used in
this book. If there are any errors or omissions, the publishers will be pleased to receive
information and will endeavour to rectify any outstanding permissions after publication.